# Song for America

*I've seen the future, brother; it is murder.*
*When they said Repent, Repent,*
*I wonder what they meant*

—**The Future,** Leonard Cohen

# Table of Contents

# Praise for *Song for America*

Using music as a powerful medium to connect the social, personal, and historical aspects of life, *Song for America*, similar to a "corrido," tells the story of a nation. Yet undeniably reminiscent of a blues song, Flores conveys feelings of oppression and pain while expressing a deep longing, highlighting the need for us to manage love and legislate against hate. 'There are no other races to conquer and no further frontiers to explore; we must make the most of what we have been given.'

> Maria Martha Chavez Brumell, Ph.D.
> President and Chief Executive Officer
> Catch the Next, Inc.

In this electrifying collection, Fernando E. Flores unleashes a symphony of verse that both honors and transcends America's poetic legacy. Each meticulously crafted line pulses with the raw heartbeat of a nation, offering revelations that startle and illuminate in equal measure. Flores doesn't merely follow in the footsteps of giants like Whitman and Roethke-he blazes a bold new trail through the American landscape, capturing its contradictions and splendor with unflinching clarity and breathtaking musicality. These poems don't just sing they soar, taking readers on a transformative journey that will forever alter how they experience poetry and the world around them. His poetry entertains and teaches, which is what great poetry should do.

> Rafael C. Castillo
> Author of *Distant Journeys*, *Aurora*,
> and *Dostoevsky on Guadalupe Street*

When I read Fernando Esteban Flores, my foot taps, heart races, mind beats-the pen the instrument of his jazz, history (our story) the light switch of his lounge. From Aztlan to San Anto and beyond, trek beside this impassioned maestro's lyrical, muscular poems-embrace the rain (the sun's sweat). America: you listening? There's a song with your name on it. *Song for America* by Hermano Fernando takes no shortcuts to redeem your soul, and not without mesmerizing it.

> Alex Z. Salinas
> Author of *The Dream Life of Larry Rios*
> and *Trash Poems*

Gnashing Teeth Publishing
242 East Main Street
Norman, AR 71960
https://gnashingteethpublishing.com

Printed in the United States of America

ISBN  978-1-966075-10-3

Non-fiction: Poetry

Gnashing Teeth Publishing First Edition

# Song for America

## I

*No tengo que asimilarme a nada. Tengo mi propia historia*—Carlos
Fuentes, novelista Mejicano

I am no one of renown
Or of importance
Just one who rose
From the violent planet
And stood amazed
At the time & place
Fate had set him in

Son of Aztlán
Not a mythic land
Or a hallucinogenic high
As historians claim
Called paradise
To keep it out of
Sight out of mind
Out of reach
America's original dream
A here & now place
I'm standing on

Hijo del sol
Mejicano
Americano

Raised from the ashes
Of a raging world
Set smack-dab in the middle
Of the nuclear age
Rocking con el ritmo
De la ciudad
Running through my veins
Rocking in my soul
Schooled by civic fables

*From sea to shining sea*
From coast to coast
Not a rags-to-riches tale
Pero un cuento de
Frijoles y arroz


From text to text
I waved the flag
Of my naïveté
Dared believe
The dream could really be
The guarantee it promised
In pursuit of liberty

Adolescence shaken
To its childish core
Before conscience
Could awaken midst
Student protests
& civil unrest
I began before it
Came undone
To clench my fists

The heroes of my youth
Were not celebrities
VIPs or bureaucrats
But personal individual
Abuelo abuela
Father mother
Sister brother
Men women
Who worked past
Social Security
& kept their word
Without complaint
They earned their worth

Unforeseen events turned
The nation's tide

Ripping the bright stars
From the bloodied stripes
Bared democracy's demagoguery
War mongers beating
Xenophobic drums

Killing Kennedys Malcolm X & King
The Gulf of Tonkin tragedy
The scourge of Vietnam
My Lai's massacre
Body bags blooming
Like a bloody business
Nixon's travesty
At Watergate
Then Iran-gate
Reagan's drama
Played out in two acts
Looting Latin America
For a grand encore
Kissinger couldn't
Sugar coat the facts

King George's Gulf War
Comus-Clinton's comedy of errors
The toppling of the
Towers & the Tyrants
Fire in the Middle East
Prince George's War on Terror

Mass destruction with impunity
The union's first black president
Emancipation proclamation never
Dared dream that far
Into the streets poor oh poor
Obama met with scorn
Blatant bigotry worn
Like a badge of honor
By those pledged
To stand as one
Politicos divvying up bile

Against minorities
Immigrants & gays

The trumpeting of trumpery
The latest craze
To raze the nation's soul
The homeland tottering
Toward apocalyptic ruin

I saw it all & sought
The poet's way
The street not chosen
Dismal & forsaken
Entered the uncertain path
No guide no ruse
Just the Muse's brew
Concocted from the
*Calles* & the blues

Among the rant and rave I
Broadcast my brand of poetry
Working class poet dissed
& dismissed for daring
Breach the pantheon
Of American lit though
I was bound to it

I stood in the place of the cyber-free
A cycloramic view of man
Mired in the customary
Chaos of the times where
The poor & the homeless roam
Subsist as bureaucratic stats
Stripped of flesh & bone
The new gods fallen stars
Cinematic-egos beamed along a million screens
To different versions of shifting truth
*Reality*-hood versus Hollywood

The true vision no longer seen
& the daily news skewers the scores

As refugees flood the venerated shores
Demonize them deport them
Bleed the country of its long blood-line
*Hands up don't shoot sal si puedes yes we can*
Double talking politicians
Homophobes xenophobes phobes of every kind
Dispute every resolution
Distort the Constitution
'Til the mind no longer minds
The new improved Jesus born too late
To save the nation from deep sown hate

*America*
Don't run don't turn away
End the age-old slant
You can't return
From where you came
Recognize your roots
Your young won't wait

I walk your familiar streets
Like an ousted foreigner
Conscious of your colonizing gaze
But every step I take a seed is set
I carry this disrupted dream
Like a bullet in the brain
A wound my life
Never recovered from
But my destiny is
*Manifest* in yours

*America*
Don't run don't turn away
You have a debt to pay
The line gets longer
& your credit doesn't rate

You cannot send us back
From where we came
Because we're right smack

In Aztlán where we began—again

✝

*The walls are the publishers of the poor*—Eduardo Galeano

At the steps of all your
Hallowed marble monuments
Washington's piercing obelisk
Lincoln on his weary throne
& the stately Jefferson
I stand like Oedipus
For all the lessons you pose
Land of sphinx & stone
Proclaiming life liberty
Happiness for all
While just a few get through

Our history tabloid of yellow crimes
Zip zap headlines inscribe the
Bloody wars our lives are
Forgotten on heaps of useless news
And yesterday's notorious views

My soul craves a home
Return to something that remains
By the dark hard streets
By the burning streams concrete
Return to first forms
Lost angry restless
Full of rage abandoned unafraid
To walk the dark & lonely road

I sing the marketable IKON
Raising millions though no
Lazarus has returned
Profitable mobile accessible MYTHS
To make the modern man dream
A WALL STREET economy
A FIFTH AVENUE Philosophy
A PLASTIC POETRY

To throw down & begin again

†

*The end of living.  The beginning of survival*—Chief Seattle

& so I stepped
Into the streets of America
A circus of smells
A comedy of terrors
A tragedy unrivalled
A cruel civility
History's mayhem

Like Aeneas newly arrived in hell
No sibyl needed to unveil
Brueghel's infernal scene
I lifted the cross of need
—no savior—
Tread the paths of my hometown
Not Palestine
Sanctified by other holocausts
Of ancestors bearing beams of broken bones

Dragging their lives like chains
Each linked in an unbroken line
Over timeless Via Dolorosas void
Of desperate Judases & weeping virgins

Each life a shrine marked on the roadside
Their dreams crushed along the way
The streets filled with fervor
& the false euphoria of belief
Faith without fire
No longer wise
The old rituals irrelevant
Religion fails the human will
Monsters of our own making
Need no conjuring
Modern infernos burn all night
The damned live here

I wandered homeless across
America's wilderness
I was no craftsman
No tradesman
No builder of any kind
A raconteur
A chronicler of times
For poets are the loveliest of liars
Who burn to paint a better world

Bootlegging poetry
Across the cultural divide
Where borders barricade
What they cannot hide
Modern cities mock the Common Man
Mere monuments to greed & gain

Who needs a poet
When idols are the fad
Who asks a poet's eyes
In an age of callous ease
Idol worship is again the rage

& I stepped onto
The city streets
The shapes & forms
The sounds of breaking
Brick & bone
The place San Anto

At Bar America
The working man
Refuels his drive
I sip a cold brew
Writing in the spaces

Between the suds
& the clack of billiard balls
Right on cue
Parting at random angles
A visual version of Big Bang

Pooling out across the green felt
Much like our lives colliding
With other spheres

Bartering for the soul of man

# Song for America

## II

*Americano Bluez*

Scenes recorded around San Antonio/for the artist, Luís López


& in the daily barter of humanity
I hear
The songs of those
Who stand outside
Your barricades
You've tried exporting dreams
& now must exorcise the dreamers


**[1:  Song of the undocumented woman & children at McDonald's]**

*Alienated in this brave new world*
*Blazing a trail with bravado*
*I advance into the future*
*Under watchful golden arches*
*On an empty stomach & bare feet*
*Pulling my progeny into forever*


**[2:  Song of two men pouring cement into wheelbarrow]**

*Pour & mix*
*Mix & pour*
*Day after day*
*Until our lives are*
*No longer ours*
*But a mixture—*
*Part concrete part blood*
*Maybe god is at the pit of the pyramid*
*Not laughing & for once looking up*

## [3:  Song of la gente laughing at a political rally at the Guadalupe Theater]

Just because the party's Democratic
Doesn't mean the people are invited
Your vote is the life of the Party
Su voto es la vida del Partido
This is no laughing matter


## [4:  Song of the construction worker with hat & one arm]

The hand that splits the rock that fuels the city
Breaks the bones that rise toward infinity
Baking stones bartering mortar for bread
An equitable trade on the New York Stock Exchange


## [5:  Song of the men with concrete blocks]

No— extraterrestrials did not teach us how to build the Pyramids
By complex measurements and back breaking toil
We squared away the sweat & the centuries' heat
The only Aliens present were the ones the politicians
Invented—the hardest work they ever did


## [6:  Song of men framing with iron]

These iron frames these ligaments & tendons
This is the body & the blood
Offered up in sacrifice to the praise & glory of the nameless—
In whose image we are made
In the Frame of the Father the Son & the Holy Ghost


## [7:  Song of Cristo-Campesino]

At the cross of the continent I stand
What's more American than the land

*Defined by work I work what's good*
*Indigenous as dirt*
*I am any man & many men*
*Pick up your shovel and follow me*

## [8: Song of two laborers with cement sacks]

*Sacks of substance*
*Seeds of sustenance*
*We hoist cities out of chaos*
*Out of cement bags & cinder blocks*
*The economy's jacked up*
*The price for dirt & earth*

## [9: Song of the apprehended undocumented workers]

*Recruited for the work our hands could yield*
*Deported for the work they said we'd steal*

*—El Corrido of the Nonessential Laborer*

An expendable market and a free enterprise nightmare

On America's Least Wanted List
Behind the Mask of Anonymity
Hides a very human face
& a heart that bleeds

## [10: Song of the man with cowboy hat putting up a wall]

*I am Atlas—Greco-Meso Titan*
*But the real myth is:*
*I hold you up so that you can stand*
*It's hard work being a god & unappreciated*

## [11: Song of the man leveling cement]

*Suffer the hard places smoothly*
*The habitat of cruelty with kindness*

## [12: Song of the man with cap resting his arm on a shovel]

*I only asked what any man*
*Would ask*
*The right to work in peace*
*To build a better life*

*Even god saw that his work was good*
*& rested on the seventh day*
*& surely must have smiled at least a little*

## [13: Song of the workers' exodus]

*O how can one dare to hope*
*When he labors in the pits of Paradise*
*O how can one dream a better world*
*When he's doomed before he dies*

# Song for America

## III

*News of one day, one afternoon, one time…*
*I believe might*
*Curry disorder in the strongest brain*
*… and perfectly demoralize the nation.*
—*World Telegram*, John Berryman

History claims its heroes
The victors' cause the right one
The rest subject to oblivion
& there are woes
Never to be solved

Time bronzed the Golden Age
Left the kiln of Chaos
To perfect what's left

†

Dallas, Texas the body of a Mexican male
Found headless & handless
His identity amputated
His destiny obliterated
Humanity mutilated

†

In this land of declarations & faith
Even the curanderos promise
Something to believe in
To stand
Against the powers of the air

In a hovel on South Presa St.
Brother Miguel offers
Powders herbs candles
To cure mal de ojo susto empacho
Out on the byways
Hunger is urgent

Voices growl
Grind
Flesh   bone

Bullets ricochet
Down alleys where
Malice never sleeps
Perdition loss
Always imminent

*Take away evil*
*Take the bus south*
Brother Miguel
Confirms the curse
Of being human

†

Una barrida cleansing
The spirit mind & body
*E Pluribus Unum* prescription
To heal the nation's
Battered & embittered soul

In this time of presidents
Not all great men are wise
Their words sound like crisp thousand-dollar bills
Bartered on The Stock Exchange for the minds of men
Their fingers brittle bones scraping empty assets
Their eyes blind to their own reflection
Covet the image splattered on video screens
Covering the bandaged eyes of Justice
In a country mapped & marked ***Democracy***

†

On the desolate southwest Texas train tracks
Four illegal Mexican immigrants
Decapitated as they slept
Sought the safety of the rails

Against the fear of rattlesnakes
The humming of the rails lulled them in a deep
Rumbling lullaby of a better life

At 17 Crystal left Austin Texas to live on her own
On October 1998 a Union Pacific worker finds her
Body in a Salt Lake City rail yard
Young cellist early high school graduate
Abandoned a college scholarship
For a life on the streets

†


Summer June 1999
Railway killer rides the Union
Pacific lines through Texas
Eludes the FBI
Suspect in 8 bloody crimes
Drifts along the railroad tracks
Hops the boxcars out of town
With rush of stealth & speed
The angel of reckoning strikes
Across the land where endless
Edicts & verdicts
Strangle justice

†


1999 Ciudad Juárez México
Hundreds of young female maquiladoras
Factory workers murdered
Their mutilated bodies dumped
In remote Mexican deserted fields
Between the cactus & coyotes
The sun bleaches their tender bones clean
The white erasure of identity
Votive candles flicker by the portraits of
Olga Adriana Sagrario
Disembodied names
Disappear in the distance like waves
Of heat on a highway bound somewhere

Silent testaments a surreal drama
Howling dogs trail the bloody sagging
Moon over the hard mountains
Desert dust covers everything

†

2011 Los Mochis Mexico cartels of choice
Wreak horrors improvise old tortures
Crack the whip of lawlessness for
The new Holy Grail demands its own
Worshippers pay more than adulation

The assailants stitched the victim's face onto
A soccer ball to state their case

†

Rural Kentucky man kills wife
Stepdaughter & three witnesses
With a shotgun then himself
Enraged over how his beloved
Cooked his eggs

†

The statue of Our Lady of Fatima
Visits San Antonio
As part of an international tour
Hard felt petrified faith
Deep in the heart of Texas

†

Columbine Virginia Tech Colorado
Newtown Connecticut Uvalde TX
The mayhem & the murder continue
19 children 2 adults killed 17 others injured
Cold blooded eighteen-year-old slayer
Venting rage & ravishing young lives
Self-appointed reaper harvesting souls

Without apparent reason or logic
The final rush of death's drug

†

Every day
The front
Page misery
Piles up

An ode to woe
A tribute to misfortune's
Splendid victories

All the news print to fit
The poetry of the age

# Song for America

## IV

*Chronicle of a Poet Foretold*

An American bio
One of millions
In the fifth decade
Of the twentieth century
A commoner's birth
Without exception
No star on the horizon
No angels hovering in the heavenlies
No kings on the periphery

Looking ahead
To the turmoil
Of the 50's & the 60's
The H-bomb's wide berth
The Korean War
The Cold War then Vietnam

Forefathers'
Chancy choice
To populate
A world they
Decolonized
By force of work

They built the railroads
Laid the tracks
Held the menial tasks
Subscribing to the dream
Lifted up the nation's flag

Father's ghost
Grandfather's shade
Give a tenuous wave
Offer up a hand to bless

As they descend their final
Resting place
They would not be company
On this northern trip

& I dropped like
A cultivated seed
In grandmother's garden
On Navidad Street
Her little white washed
Corner lot house
I would grow
A prickly weed
Among scorpions
& horned toads

As wars crisscrossed the globe
Battles thundered all around
I emerged wounded
By loss
Questionably—whole—

Humane
By destiny's intent
Bent to the larger world
My tribe—I claim
Raised under fallen stars & bloody stripes

Their war was not my war
My fight not theirs
& yet together tossed
By broiling world events

Toward one end
Blends our lives
Blurs our lines
Of demarcation

†

One day one year
More or less

These poems
Will pave the streets
Bits of dust
Flattened by the meticulous
Machines of modernity
A crumbling tribute
To a transient humanity
Worn smooth beneath
The steps I took
Over the city
Of the poet I became
There is no refuge for men like me
The world in all its raggedness is
Sole sanctuary
At Bar America
I take communion
With the men & women of the streets
Fellow celebrants
In this solitary passage
Moving together
In solidarity
Yet quite alone

Here we script
Our own survival

# Song for America

## V

*Yo soy San Antonio*

I sing of you San Antonio
Slumming along the railways
Kicking the flinty rocks
Down the sweltering tracks
Fired by Tonatiuh's relentless rays
I find you simmering in
The dog days' doggedness
La canicula as ancianos still say

Miles & piles of railroad ties south by southwest
Where Abuelo staked
His soul in dirt & sweat
Linking his progeny to the future
So that I'd always be
On my way somewhere

Yanaguana—
Refreshing waters—
To the Coahuiltecans
Original Texans

Conceived in 1691 for Spain
On the feast day of St. Anthony of Padua
A.K.A. Fernando Martins de Bulhões my namesake
Mi tocayo venerated worldwide as the patron saint of all things lost
For who can say what comes to find
Its place among your roots

City of Franciscan missions & presidios
Capistrano
San José
Concepción
Espada
San Antonio de Valero
In their search for gold

The Spaniards
Left a gilded litany
Of feeble saints & you—a jewel—
Among their embattled settlements

We know you
By marks along the routes
Men have made to risk their claim
For fame or notoriety

City of rebels
Crockett Bowie Travis
Transplanted Texians
Of Ricardo y Enrique Flores Magón
Sons of anarchy provocateurs de la revolución
Hijos de Mejico hijos del sol

City of odd & antiquated foreignness
Noted a renowned Central Park architect
Built upon native & mestizo blood
Your river treks a long slow
Stretch homeward
To the Gulf of Mexico

City of creeks mesquites
Scrub land flatland
Brambles & caliche roads
Bordered by skin & bony barrios
Blue moons & red conjunto nights

On Frío City Road
Union Pacific boxcars
Still rail down the tracks
Scarring the fringe of the western barrio
Like an old switchblade gash
From a back-street fight

Growing up
No one ever bothered

To explain
Its rough translation

Harsh existences chiseled out
& crushed along a jagged rip
Of pavement spanning
More than fifty years

At the red-brick
Roegelein Meat Packing Company
Minimum wage Mexicans
Packed their sweat & dreams
Into the sausage casings that fed the city

Corridor of dilapidated bars
Razed by recessions
Rise under new management
To the same old Yankee Doodle

Empty houses become churches
Become empty again
As the flames of revival fade
Year in year out

At the urban renewed
Alazan-Apache projects
Men surround a Coleman ice chest
Drinking away destiny
As corridos from Los Tigres del Norte
Fuel their obsession
Toasting to the next
One hundred years of servitude

Tecato & syringe street
Only the Mo-Pac lines
Offer escape beyond
The blood stench
Of the Union Stockyards
& the slaughterhouses
Where for decades
The snarl of bestial death

Was ritual as the stabbings
& shootings beneath
Highway 90 West

One came to expect
On certain nights
When the breath
Of stale Pearl beer
Scoured the belly
Of the serpent underfoot

Coiling its long finger grip
Around each
Concrete citizen
Of the streets

From St. Anthony de Padua
Where I was baptized
Into a church I abandoned
For lack of a better faith
& left the flock
To find another fold

To Catedral de San Fernando
The fire of devotion burning
In Abuela's hopeful eyes
The candle of fidelity
Unwavering to the end of her days
Certain that her trust would be redeemed
Her right hand raised in beatific blessing
Bestowing her benevolence
As she gestured the sign of the cross
Over her children's children

& who now remembers the Alamo
Shrine to two clashing ideals
Owned by other impresarios
With vested interests not our own
Controlled as a commodity

The ghosts of fallen soldiers bartered for a token
El Degüello echoing through the plaza as we dispassionately pass by

This is where the roulette stops
City where I post my posterity
Raise the flag of all my precedents
The place partitioned
From birth to be my lot
This geographical genome
At once sacred & profane
I am you yo soy San Antonio

America—
Land of conviction
& contradiction
I stake my claim
& aim to make
Your declarations true

As foreign to indigenous
Though you perceive me alien
You can't strip the stars above me
I've paid the price
I bore the dream
Though you doubt
I'm here at home
A place I never left
Dreaming a life
I'm living in

Destiny in the blood
Of those who strive
To forge a better way
You can no more renounce me
Than I denounce you
I fashion no false notions
Make no idols of your words
There are wrongs to right
Unmask & assert our identity
Bear up or fade away
History ever at our side

# Song for America

## VI

*A Lesson in Texas History* or *How Mexico Lost the War*

A poem without Mexicans for Ken Burns, producer of documentary films

El Alamo
Was no
Thermopylae
Though the tragedy
Was epic
Greek
& thus, classic

No
Three hundred Spartans or so
Leonidas vs. Xerxes' 10,000 Immortals
Eat well for the next meal will be in hell
Leonidas is said to have said
Before he losing his head

Yes,
History always favors the select
It's never kind to losers or rejects
So the textbooks Texans have recorded
Straight—out of pulp fiction

Just
A ragtag team of surging insurgents
Not quite the elite Hoplites of SPARTAN fame
Wanting to invoke self-liberty
Secede from old world Mejico
Right off the pages of Machiavelli

Where those on THIS side go
When they want a little toot
Or a naughty walk on the wild side
Which doesn't apply now

For those on THAT side
So right wing bigots turn loose
The political juice
& fences go up
Immediately
On the nightly news

All this ritz:
Tailor made for
Hollywood glitz

Satanize Santa Anna
& all his boys
Become bandidos
To neutralize the score

An Academy Award
O for Oscar starring *the Duke*
Plus the juke box track
Á la Marty Robbins'
Ballad of the Alamo

Growing up TEX—but
Being MEX—
We were a tad—
MIXed up

Did we root for who we were
Wishing that we weren't?
Wanting coonskin caps & flintlocks

Screw the facts:
3,000 or so versus 180
What are facts anyway?
Trivial things that stand or fall
In a Bexar County court of law

Depending on what side
Of the Rio Grand you're from
& what skin you find yourself locked in
Before you get the boot—

Moot now
But Santa Anna toyed
With the Texian boys.
Ooo-la-la
 Á la Napoléon
For 13 days
Before sounding
El Degüello
No mercy mercy me
For the sons of Tennessee
& the rebels fell
To fight another day

At San Jacinto
The Defenders of the Faith
Struck a back blow
For oil wells and Taco Bell

Bowie Travis Bonham Crocket
Replaced the mestizo sons of the Aztec
As the official Elect
Empresarios of the barrios

Yet, the Daughters of the Republic declined
An interview on the grounds
That they must maintain the hollow
Shrine of Texas Liberty

So we come here not to *praise Caesar*
*But to bury Him*

For men must make their stand
Demarcations drawn in legendary sand

& History says so very few are honorable

# Song for America

## VII

### Blues for The American Dream

Poem on the wall at the Delta Produce building at S. Brazos and S. Laredo Streets
recently painted over

Did you dream the American dream
Was it a tale told by an idiot

Full of myth
Full of lies
Full of laughter
Full of cries

Did you dream the American dream
Was it a Hollywood movie for the big screen

Was it glitzy
Was it gory
Did it win an Oscar
Or a Grammy

Did you dream the American dream
Was it dollar green

Where all the fat cat piggies
Rake in all the cash
All the pink & tickled piggies
Piling up their stash

Did you dream the American dream
Is it just an elephant & donkey's game

Who will win
Who will lose
Who will sing
The barrio blues

Did you dream the American dream
Did it all get lost somehow

Can you find it on the Westside
Up on Zarzamora Street
Down on Frío City Road
Where all the homies meet

Is the American dream
All they said it'd be

Read about it in a book
Watch it on MTV
An idea too good to be true
For folks like you & me

What color is freedom
How much does liberty cost

Is it worth the sweat & pain
When so many have been lost
The price is stamped in blood
Waiting in your name

# Song for America

## VIII

### I Hear America Cringing

No apologies to Walt Whitman

I hear America cringing

The barbaric venom laced rhetoric across the continent of discontent
The poor each one cringing from the emptiness of blunted promises
The unemployed cringing as they measure out their last mortgage payment
    wondering
Where to go after it's all gone

The unwed mother cringing as she struggles to make ends meet day after day
    looking at her
Unborn torn with uncertainty
The battered wife & mother running for her life wondering how this came
    to be
The drug addicted cringing in the streets scouring the city for a quick health
    care fix

The abandoned children cringing in the land of the free with leftover dreams
    to eat
The victims of violence cringing in dread as they hold their wounded or their
    dead listening to those who violently defend the right to kill
The homeless at the end of their rope looking for a different day that doesn't
    start with a curse or
Shredded hope

The dispirited mistreated arrested & jailed for being a darker shade of pale
The wounded vets with no regrets asking only what was signed be delivered
The immigrants cringing in disbelief at the hate they meet at Lady Liberty's
    gates—her denizens
Shouting slurs and slime
The politician's paradox cringing at the thought—statesmanship or
    salesmanship

A nation running out of choices cringing in a sea of prosperity mired in
        perplexity
Truths self-evident or partisan bullshit

America cringing in the balance of it all

# Song for America

## IX

Though we leave our place
Of birth behind with empty bellies
Tired feet & little hope
Of ever seeing loved ones again
Swimming the Río Grande
Walking long stretches
Over blistering sand
Riding el tren de la muerte—*La Bestia*
Or cram into trucks & trailers
Praying we make it undetected
Each paying all we have
Maybe more
*El coyote* says we'll be
Taken care of once we cross
Over rivers canyons deserts mountains
Where they spit on us call us aliens
Wetbacks illegal immigrants
Undocumented
Terrorists they yell but
The only terrorists we see
Are angry men with loaded guns
Pointed at our foreheads
Not once do they say
Human beings
We lose family friends
When it's our turn
Which way's home
We run al otro lado
the other side
Some get through
But never arrive

# Song for America

## X

### For the dreamers

I sing not an ode
Masked in an eloquent mode
I merely ask the Muse to bless these
Inner city blues

For those who know not peace
Or lives of ease
Or the glory of such nights as these
Who stand fast

While others act so callously
With casual regard for liberty
Who can't give voice
To suffering or words to grief

Who only watch
Their lives X-ed out
By the menial things
The world imparts

Spend their days toiling
In poverty 's workshop
Never knowing surplus
Mired in the pits

Not daring the heights
Spend their nights
In cold dark places
Warmed by empty wishes

With neither choice nor chance
Victims of undocumented change
Condemned to a forever after
Without benefit

I celebrate those who live with less
Whose meager existence
Ensures another's' excess—
Who never realize
A better tomorrow
Fleeing yesterday's
Inescapable horror
Who will never win
A Nobel Prize

Written off after birth
To an unequivocal worth

This elegy—

A *nobler* prize

# Song for America

## XI

*When bullets kiss the tenderest flesh*

Brown or black or some other darker shade of pale
A hail of gunfire never fails to find its mark
Shattered tendons bones muscle sown at birth
When dreams as yet unclear showed then more promise
When every soul was priceless at its highest worth
Before ill choice or chance snuffed out the fires of hope
The riddled bodies on the ruthless streets pile up these days
The method's madness authorized by those who know
The reasons given never match the questions raised
& blame—the easiest game to play

*When bullets kiss the tenderest flesh*

Who stems the splattered blood
Who binds the open wounds
Who repairs the irreparable
Who dares to reach the place
That harbors human hate
The means that justified the ends
Enough surpassed more than enough
Who feels no pain when hurt
Who knows no loss when lost
Who does not bleed or pay the cost

*When bullets kiss the tenderest flesh*

# Song for America

## XII

*In Praise of the Second Amendment*

Who ignores the requiem
For Sandy Hook Columbine Colorado
Uvalde Texas
Who can hold a wounded life
Between his arms & be unaffected

Children cut off before their prime
—such a small catastrophe—
The rest keep ragging at iniquity
Before a blind bewildered justice

*How to curb the violence*
Zealots respond *is to take up arms*
The elect promote so little reason
Politics offers so much less

Where to find the fix
In such an expeditious age
Where data travels at the click
Of the electronic page

Can it mean anything
To anyone when
Poets point out
What others often miss

If offering poems
Could stem the bleeding
But the killing does not stop
& not a single soul seems safe

# Song for America

## XIII

The brown child behind the chain link fence of aborted dreams
Wishes warm food new clothes & days without hate laced looks

The 21-year-old undocumented immigrant hears rumors of
College a good job & days without glancing over his shoulder

The immigrant mother & father beseech the saints for
Work a good home & waking once to good news

The Bible toting verse exporting politician screams of
The day he can *damn them all to hell*

# Song for America

## XIV

Inmate #40288-115 speaks

Civil rights civil unrest
The 70's cauldron of distrust & discontent
All along the American watchtower
Disconnect from the body politick
The government swore to uphold
Conspiracies to dull the conscience
Of democratic power
History tells a better tale with time

"I sought a level playing field
For the working poor
Mejicano laborers
In the southern fried Texas fields
For nickels & dimes
Not much change left
After taxes and bills
I, too, plotted there as a boy
Up at 6 a.m. to pick 1,000 pounds a day
Mom sweating alongside the rest
Pulling a 12-foot cotton sack
A quick tortilla no lunch
Barely back at dusk for a late snack"

"Later a scholarship to Baylor
And a Juris Doctor Degree
Made the dream real for me at twenty-nine
I became the youngest candidate for governor
In the Lone Star State 1973
Alma Canales my chosen running mate
For the first time in South Texas
Hispanic Texans had a choice
Lift their voice in unity
Be heard in a state where
Mexicans were politically
& legally marginalized

To know their rightful place
High stakes for a fledgling La Raza Unida Party
Shook Governor Dolph & the Democrats
Down to their custom-made ostrich boots
Hard-liners took a long serious note
None will ever know the plans discussed in caucus
But the bottom fell out fast
After a brief star burst
A one count felony drug conspiracy charge
& a 15-year fix at a federal penitentiary
Brought the whole Party to an end in '76
Disbarred & disgraced I was released
In five from the federal pen
Only to face trumped up cocaine
Charges in a DEA sting
Was this a classic backroom plot
Or a dirty deal gone wrong
Sentenced to life without reprieve"

"Innocence seems absurd to claim this late
Were it not my plea to break
The chains of subtle bigotry
In '71 Lieutenant William Calley
Murdered twenty-two Vietnamese civilians
Served 3 years under house arrest
Pardoned by ex-Presidente Nixon
Justice dealt out a sympathetic hand
While I suffer Time's stiffest fine"

*My name is Ramsey Muñiz, inmate 40288-115*
*I reside in the barbaric state of Leavenworth*

# Song for America

## XV

### *American History*

*Good Queen Bess* agreed
Profits prevailed so set sail
The *Good ship Jesus* alongside
*The Amistad Desire the Elizabeth*

Yanked a nation to its knees
Dropped their contraband
Upon a young continent
Privatized opportunity

The ships' manifests list
Mulattoes—people
Of color—fettered
To a life in chains

Jewish merchants
Moses & Mordecai reaped
The first proceeds of
Slave ships bound

For Portugal
France Spain
England North
America

The Age of Science Discovery
The Industrial Revolution
Drove the long steely blade
Of greed cloaked as destiny

Into a fledgling country's soul
Baptized in the blood of innocents
Not one founding father
Stopped Cruelty's steeped hands

There the masters
Of the Constitution
In love with words
Getting it all in writing

Creating the GRAND INSTITUTION
The national record ranks
Crimes of historical dimension
Points to pious hands

The sad denizens
Living on the brink
Before the ink
On declarations dried

Could only try
To make sense of
What it all meant

With all the talk
Of treaties rights
& those created in the likeness
Of some strange god

Who hung upon
A cross of wood
*A violent death*
They said for their creator's son

Who spoke of love
& peace on earth
Who now demanded
Punishment on anyone

Deemed not worthy
Of his approving trust
& thus they strung
So many undeserving lives

From unsuspecting trees

Signs to those who would resist
& up for grabs came
Land & goods

Appropriated
To a few select
Who declared the
Indigenous evicted


No ballot
No vote
Their welfare
Broke

Bullets erased
Complaints
Silenced
Dissent

Freedom spent
On dreams
Of those in chains
Their only choice

Submit
Survive
Or disappear
But where was there to go

The country parceled out
Piecemeal pursuing profit
Thus birthed *The American Way*

Life Liberty Equality
Crack the whip with a weary beat
No part of the public text
For the dark man on the street

An entire country billed
Crimes against humanity

A task for a Homer
Or another Dante
—an epic undertaking for a burgeoning poet

Folding his glasses rubbing his forehead
Thinking the national blotter
Points one way but
Memory runs in another

& a bloated corpse goes on bleating

# Song for America

## XVI

*For a native son*

Upbeat not beat
*Fired up & ready to go*
Eight years of political discord
Berated about his birth
His name mocked
Religion suspect
Upbraided for his youth and aloofness
Thwarted at each step
Threatened with malicious violence
Obstructed by disruptive malcontents
Intent on insult & ill will
Caricatured lampooned
Butt of racial jokes
The greatest republic
In the history of the world
Fixated on vulgarity
You would have thought
They'd tout another native son
For all the good he'd done
Who's after all as much American
As Washington and Jefferson
Still his wit his sanity held
With a hop in his step
Audacious hope undimmed
An infectious smile
The light in his eyes never brighter
Did his job bid his time
Said goodbye waved farewell
Moving ahead
Even if alone

For all the opposition raised
The hatred the bitterness
Opportunities missed that
come only once
A thousand possibilities lost
America all the lesser for it

# Song for America

## XVII

*Some Bad Hombres*
—Donald Trump

Leap tall border walls
In a single bound
Bolt America's buildings
Build America's railroads
Glean America's crops
Wash iron mop sweep
Keep America squeaky clean
Tend America's gardens
Construct America's homes
Collect America's garbage
Service America's cars
Sweat in America's factories
Wait on America's tables
Fight in America's wars
Die in America's wars
Steal American jobs
Snubbed American citizenship
Dubbed the welfare class
Called criminals & rapists
Dark & undesirable
American as dirt

*Those are some bad hombres*

# Song for America

## XVIII

### Impressions on the Inauguration of the 45th President of the United States

Can't shake the
Feeling we're
At a wake or
At a morgue
Waiting for
A corpse to be
Wheeled in
For a crime
That hasn't
Been committed yet
So the body
Can be brought in
Properly attended
& mourned

But we're not alone
There are others
Here with us
Some sit in silence
Too stunned to speak
Others shout angry
Curses to the air
A few dab
Their watery eyes
One or two
Vow to fight
Resist at any price
Most of us
Feel helpless
Rubbed raw inside
Unfocused
Out of sorts
Lost

As if someone
Dear has reached out
To us but now
Has passed
& we—too late—
Can only
Watch & wait
Outside
People trumpet
Nasty slogans
To energize
Their partisans
Others yell
In protest
Howl louder
Break storefront
Windows
Set cars
On fire
Hold signs
Scream their dire discontent
Into the TV screen

The pomp & ceremony
Echoing the treacherous streets
The circumstances funereal
All too shady
All too familiar

# Song for America

## XIX

*U.S. military drops "Mother of All Bombs" in Afghanistan*

They announced today as if
The greatest triumph
Of mankind had occurred
Somehow in reverse
Men birthed the *Mother of All Bombs*
MOAB so named
11 tons of explosives
Unleashed in Afghanistan
Profaning mothers of their worth
Delivered unto us
April 13, 2017
As we woke up
To greet the morning news
Gawking at the TV screen
Did the fathers cheer
Their progeny
Did they pass around the
Customary cigars
& pat each other
On the back
For a job well done
Delivering Death Destruction & Defeat
Like gold frankincense & myrrh
Upon suspect terrorists
& unsuspecting mothers
Children fathers
As the world grows safer
Each & everyday

# Song for America

## XX

*Words matter*


They mill about like foreigners at customs' gates
Waiting for the chance to prove their worth
Hoping you take notice as a friend
Or somehow wave them on in
Credentials probed & calibrated
A jumbled mass they wait
The crude might be of use
The *laissez-faire* slim odds of getting through
The sweet ones pinch like two tight shoes
Others calculate a slight tactical edge
An aural nip or a visual plus
Perhaps strike a pun
Or a double entendre
That will push them over
Well ruled delineated borders
Still some appear too questionable
Their curlicues or serifs
Chipped or broken off
Veterans of many literal
Fictional & military wars
Verbal TNT too volatile to trust

They ask no quarter bread or drink
Only to be mobilized
Utilized in a humane way
A substantial lexicon—no doubt
Disposed to be deployed
Entire genealogies backed up
For blocks at your fingertips
Etymologies rooted in ancient towns
Encyclopedias to be plundered on a whim
The moment under siege
You must choose
You must redress

The many messages
Each one texts
Dare share
Sacred space
How & what to mix
Each word a risk

# Song for America

## XXI

### Memorial Day memory

*Say adiós so long*
*Jesús Rosalio Roberto León*

Father tíos friends
Others of our honored dead

Shields of my early life
Buried underneath the vast Texas skies

Each wrapped in the flag of country
Fought for de todo corazón—all heart

Believing it would give you
Some hope a place to start

Living out that scene cited in those
Spartan classrooms of your American youth

Though not readily received
In the land of your own birth

Of humble second-class worth
By virtue of the palette your skin

You ground your fingers in &
To the bone to stake your place

Among the jagged stripes & sweeping stars
Looking down the long barrel of

Battles you gave your innocence for
Green & wet behind the ears

What did you know of world affairs
Behind your brown & scrawny frames

Young boys barely men from small
Pueblitos dusty little South Texas towns

Off you went odds against to test your verve
& back you came shaken yet undeterred

Each one having braved the worst
That men can do to other men in war

The first of families to have
Dared risk the only goods

You had to barter with
& then pull off the improbable

& moved the rest of us a little further
Up to dream bigger than before

I listen for the meaning now
As mournful *Taps*

Bugles out its measured notes
Of unmeasured pain

Across the nation's
Hallowed grounds

Fort Sam Laredo
San Fernando Arlington

Where you lie in state
This remembered day

Knowing you gave your best
As men can do

I honor you though long past due
Father uncles dearest friends

May we meet again
As we were meant

*So long* I say *adios*

# Song for America

## XXII

### History Lesson

This is the song of a country
Built on the backs of slaves
With the blood & sweat
Of the indigenous
The song of the living
The song the dead

♪ *Mine eyes have seen the glory of the coming of the Lord;*
*He is trampling out the vintage where the grapes of wrath are stored;*
*He hath loosed the fateful lightning of His terrible swift sword:*
*His truth is marching on…*♪

Chains at the ankle
Yoke at the neck
Manacled to the ship
The horrible cries
The human waste
The stale air soiled
By the vomit stench
Thick with groans
Death moans
Of the sick
Whip & lash
To subdue defiant
Men women children
Kidnapped from their lands
Dragged against their will
Sold inhuman bondage
The battle hymn
Of the republic
The new language

When the English ship
—*The White Lion*—

Disembarks at Jamestown
1619 with "20 & odd" Africans
Scripted in the record
Custom soon becomes law
Law hangs out its shiny shingle
On America's front lawn
Launches its practice branding
Those pristine souls whose calamity
Became the color of their skin

♫ *Glory, glory, hallelujah*
*His truth is marching on…* ♫

Shackled marches
Forced internment
*Nu na da ul tsun yi*
(the place where they cried)
As the Cherokee called it
Exposure disease starvation
The nation's gift for their
Compliant cooperation
& peaceful capitulation

America's natal citizens
Held hostage taken prisoner
Dragged toward a fatal oblivion
Their lands impounded
Their culture decimated
America's first notorious aliens
The new legal residents

♫ *O beautiful for spacious skies,*
*For amber waves of grain*
*For purple mountain majesties*
*Above the fruited plain*
*America  America* ♫

1830 Congress kicks off
Its much-feted campaign
The forcible removal
Of indigenous tribes

From ancestral lands
The U.S. army herds them like cattle
Bound for the beauty of the Rez
In the name of a civilized nation
The right of conquest the sole aim
Total annihilation
The behest of the new masters
Who watch the endless trail of tears
& turn away

♫ *Señora Santa Ana por que llora el niño*
*Por una manzana que se le ha perdido* ♫
♫ *...& the yellow Rose of Texas*
*shall be mine forever more* ♫

Leaving Laredo Texas
Mother would always stress
*"Say you are a U.S. citizen*
*When the Border Patrol agent asks*
*Where you're from boy?"*
*"How cum we'd say?"*

Then squirm in our seats
Rubbing our skin
Wondering why
I would've told him
Father was a WWII vet
Purple Heart pinned to his chest
Later I would say
With a sarcastic bit
*USA all the way*
The agent in turn would twitch
& cast a shifty glance
Before he nodded the ok

La Hora de Sangre Texas 1848
The Time of Blood the massacre
At Porvenir Presidio County
Texas Rangers round up 15 residents
March them off to rocky bluffs

& execute them promptly on the spot
Presuming they were
Spies for Pancho Villa
Widows & forty-five orphans
The spoils of the day
Lynching Mejicanos
Continue through the 1920s
Stores post signs in San Antonio
Snarling *No dogs or Mexicans allowed*
Mob rule the new sheriff in town
In a country of convenient shifty laws

Brown in its richest roasted shades
Earthen tones of every land form
The latest symbol of low worth
Incites the colonizers' hate
Mass incarceration absconding abolition
The only means to an overt end
& Death decked out in pious robes
Dispenses impartial righteousness

The revolution each foreign looking face
Through every border fence
Staring so much further up ahead
Reminding you how much
The nation lost from
What it sought to gain

This is the song of a country
A song you can't get out
Of your head
Destined to repeat
Till you forcibly forget the words
& whistle the tune instead
The nightmare you can't waken from
The one you will remember
When you get out of bed

A country
Built on the backs of slaves
With the blood & sweat

Of the indigenous
Of the indigent

Song of the living
Song of the dead
Song of the love
I sing

♫ *God Bless America*
*My home sweet home*♫

# Song for America

## XXIII

the nation's anthem

If I stand
Or if I kneel
What does that reveal
Of the Nation's state—
The flag flies half staff
For our endangered species
No disrespect
For country
No malice toward
Those who gave their lives
In her defense
No hatred for those
Who sacrificed
What they had
That the machinery of democracy
Could go on

If I stand
Or if I kneel
The heart protests
The subtle lies
The political palaver
Of those who govern
For their gain
& stand before the flag
With two faced hands over shady hearts

The heart rebels against
The systemic wrongs
Poured out upon
The poor & powerless
The heart resists
The pointed blade of prejudice
The heavy hammer of oppression
The cold sickle of aggression

Unleashed by those sworn to
Keep the peace
The heart rejects
The cruel attempts
To suffocate
The voice of the oppressed
If I stand
Or if I kneel
The heart will not fail
Cower or bow
Before the walls of tyranny
Petty despots build
Wielding their arms
Of cowardice hate fear
Sanctified & wrapped
In orchestrated stars & stripes
Dangling their false brands
With jingoistic jingles
Meant to numb the brain
Dull the heart

Pero el corazón no traicionará
Su propia verdad sagrada

But the heart will not betray
Its own sacred truth

Aunque por mil años
En cadenas espere

Though in chains it waits
A thousand years

# Song for America

## XXIV

*Heavy Metal Man*

If I should shed one ounce of blood
Upon the killing fields
Let it be to build a place for peace

Let my life be one of use
To mark my path in my own way

For the strength to stand
For what I am
A heavy metal man

Full iron tempered will
Steel against steel
Turning back the dark Titans of Time

To stand still
& not to yield

If I should dream but one true dream
Let it be the hope of all
For all to dream

To build with hands the myths
To see with eyes the vision

Of the future like a phoenix rise
Out of the broken bloodied world
Spanning spiraling a boundless sky

If I should live but one true life
Let it be to fight for the right to be
Free of any ideology
Of ignorance of hate & of defeat

To stand for what I am
A heavy metal man

# Song for America

## XXV

*The United States themselves are essentially the greatest poem.*
—Walt Whitman

the Outcasts

Where O Walt Whitman
Bard of universal man
Blaze the democratic vistas of your vision
Where lies the largesse of the nation the simplicity of its soul
Where hides its ingenuity
Where resides its heroic hospitality
Who sings the vastness of its great psalm
*Where is the man of letters where is the book*
To script the scope & span of this great land

Only the streets grant sanctuary these days
Offer a sense of hope & openness
Better than the *better life* publicized
Up ahead with signs that say
*We reserve the right*
Denied a Bienvenida meaning
Not welcome here

Out on Frío City Road Guadalupe Street
Buena Vista Commerce
Where the dark men meet
Lining the alleys
Loitering the tracks
Hunched together
American outcasts
Seeking refuge
Without direction
Home—downtown
Wherever our feet can stand

Hunger clawing at the bones
A shuffling subsistence

The city bummed
With mechanized men
Scraping out a fix among the ruts
Beneath the freeways
Littered with card box dreams
Habitués of habit addicted
To the next trumped-up deal
Of empty pockets picked clean
Rummaging the garbage dumps
Of misery & regret
The doors to a rusted paradise
Of souls starved into despair
Rotting under a dead pan moon
The law of survival
Rules the place you wish
You could remember
An abstraction a blur
The Grand American expression
Poetry *kosmical* & bold
Folded in your wallet
Crumpled from neglect

The streets your avatar
Beckoning your return
The past a dilapidated democracy
A spoof of what you wanted
Singer of *Self*
You were only looking
For a way into this place
Walt Whitman
In love with the idea
Called *America*
Before walls
Partitioned off the land
& people became a means to an end

Country of convenient borders
Barbed wire barricades
For those who with blood & brawn
Hoisted up the steel scaffolds of trade
The arterial lines of transport

The clanging iron riveting
The skeletal frame in place
The jackhammers breaking down stone
With blood & brow
Forever nameless faceless
Standing on the outskirts
Looking straight ahead
At a home that never was
A land where freedom rings
From a fenced in lot
Promoting a plastic posterity
On the way to the republic Walt
Words topple walls poems lessen the load we all must bear
Let us go out you & I into the barrios of this land
Our feet upon the open road

# Song for America

## XXVI

*Jazz-icity*

*Jazz is restless. It won't stay put and it never will.* –trombonist J. J. Johnson

Thundering 'mid
        Crashing cymbals

Blaring brass
        Sustaining syncopation

Atonal conflagration
        Crossed twentieth century America

Cruising south
        Booming down the East coast

Moving West
        At the speed of groove

Great swell of swinging sound
        Tsunami of spontaneous harmony

Zipzappin' zeboppin'
        The USA in a home-grown Chevrolet

Zoom
    Zoom
        Zoom of the highways & the byways
Beat
    Beat
      Beat of the city streets

Hum
    Drum
        Thrum of everyday life

Funkified junk
        Honk & squeal

Alive with a thousand
                Shafts of aqueous light

Toetappin'
        Footstompin'
                Beboppin'

From Harlem
        To Guadalupe street

Shuffle & shake
        At the Blue Note or the Five Spot

The air inhaled
        The tones exhaled

Light that never fails
        To smooth your darkest night

The hearts that break
        The love that's made

The blood streaming
        Through the open veins

Of this American dream
        Red white & oh so, blue

*Kind of Blue*
        *Blue in Green*

Smiles & Miles
        *Take the A-train* to Coltrane

Birdland *Alice's Wonderland*
        Mingus to Thelonious

Xylophone to saxophone
        Days that rock nights that roll

Flo-etry in the poetry
             The Bird & the word

*It ain't the meat it's the motion*
             *How deep is the ocean*

The dangle of the angle
             The stars the spangles

True grit tasty grits
             *Fried neck bones & some home fries*

Beans & cornbread
             *Tortillas y frijoles borrachos*

Spanish grease *Manteca*
             Served up *bien sabroso*
*Watermelon Man*
             Willie Bobo Mongo y Poncho
Bongos-n-congas
             Suburbs to slums

Boroughs to barrios
             Land of a thousand dances

& all the chances one can ever hope to take
             *Body & Soul Papa was a Rolling Stone*

Sonny Stitt *Salt and Pepper*
             Art Pepper Jelly Roll

Josephine Baker Chet Baker
             Tatum's *Perdido*

Parker *in Paris*

        *Autumn in New York*

American born

        From a brazen brass horn

LA to SA all points beyond

        Flowing with such long longing

The air you need

        The sounds that sate

Your restless soul

        The sure voice of revolution

Liberty's true anthem

        Jazz

# Song for America

## XXVII

### Reflections on September 11, 2001

Many wonder what will happen next
Many predict the predictable end of all
& all eyes look toward the Middle East
Where holy terror wears an ordinary face

These are times that make believing hard
But we've come to these roads before
Where one way imposes its will
& many lives are sacrificed to that cold god

Who hides behind the words of ancient texts
Only few can understand that Will to
Rain destruction on unsuspecting infidels
Like men & women whose only sin
Was to wish their loved ones well

Before rushing off to meet their fate
In an unexpected place where another
Flaming sun was waiting to be met
& faith fell through a hell of twisted steel

Now many wonder what will happen next
Many unpredictable things must not be loosed
All eyes must look into each heart
Where peace must find its way again

# Song for America

## XXVIII

for Marvin Gaye

Nobody knows
It's absolutely so
After Lincoln
After the lynching
After Kennedys & King
After Malcolm X & Mohammed Ali
After picket sign protest lines
After riots Civil Rights Voting Rights
After sit-ins & love-ins
Marching a million miles for peace
After the horrid wars that never cease
After *X* number of deaths
After the bans against people
After crimes against humanity
After exile & asylum
After immigration exploitation
After gun violence escalation
After mass deportations
After family separations
After calls for border walls & tariff wars
After the entire planet is a time bomb
Ticking in Times Square

Long after Marvin Gaye sang
*Only love can conquer hate*
The answer so absurdly clear
We learned to turn the other cheek
And in return received an implacable deaf ear

Even those who think they do
No one's sure Nobody knows

Lies bleach truth
Truth leaches lies
Facts birth fakes
Fakes sprout false things
With feathers
That cannot fly
The rich grow hip
The poor get zip
Traitors hailed patriots
Patriots proclaimed traitors
Allies enemies
Enemies allies
Haters are lovers
Lovers are haters
Zeroes the heroes
Heroes the zeroes
The White House the outhouse
*E pluribus unum* united in one hate
America takes its rightful place

& those who should know
Know they don't
No one knows
What's going on

# Song for America

## XXIX

for the students from Margory Stoneman Douglas High School & the March for Our Lives movement, San Antonio, TX July 10, 2018 at La Trinidad United Methodist Church

Across the country from cities soaked with blood of friends & family
Young survivors of gun violence on high school campuses
Gather at La Trinidad Church to share
Their concerns promoting conversation & "common sense" solutions
For the bloodshed plaguing the nation
Meet patriotic men of few words
Who wouldn't hesitate to shoot first
If skin got in the way of a bullet's thirst
Men who'd rather debate with semi-automatic weapons in their hands
While parroting the party line of thin half truths

The young have heard the argument before
Many more times than their youth belies
The look on their faces says they aren't buying a word
They argue life is a sacred right
They want to grow & live
The man patting a holstered gun among a group of armed men
Makes his point emphatically clear he
Is here to ensure that *his* rights are not "slowly stripped away"
& the gun securely strapped to his waist defends his right

The Second Amendment—fought so hard to keep—
Can safely sleep tonight
Tucked away in the hallowed pages of U.S. history 101
Knowing guns do not kill people
People kill people

# Song for America

## XXX

Blues for Zarzamora Street
Friday, July 13, 2018

1

Zarzamora Street dark as an overripe
Blackberry ready to drop long overdue
Offers up its store of bruised fruit
Neon dots the side streets
Like candles in holy pilgrimage
The way over flowering with
Saints & sinners
Auto shops fast food joints
Gas stations convenience stores
Cell phone shops selling more
Hardware than we'll ever need
Wichos Mexican Deli odd for
A restaurant this side of town
Named for the "Richards" that made it out
& those that never left
*Sombras* Night Club
Where the singer belts out in a gruff voice
*Una cruz de madera de las más corriente*
Then segues into *la rama del mesquite*
Y *la vida y la muerte* go spinning 'round
The dance floor *como la rueda de la fortuna*
& where she stops nobody knows
*La poesía del pueblo* breaking out in all
Its earthy forms mixed with
The sweat & toil of its people

2

Buildings crowd the corners
Like sellers at a flea market
Vying for your attention
& your vanishing dollar bills
Young mothers push baby

Carriages past danger laced alleys
Gambling with dimes for diapers
A man & woman embrace under a tangle of
Telephone wires melting into each other
A single flame symbol of *amor eterno*
In such a temporal place
Muffled men shuffle north & south
In single file on cramped walks
No room to chart a course
& a wrong way glance a one way ticket
To the ER or worse
DPS troopers cop cruisers trail
Scraggly perps into unlit paths
The nightly ritual dogging the needy
The oldest barrios of the city not affluent
Enough or of any influence to be marked historical
On an empty lot people plaster the dilapidated wall
Of a confiscated Acapulco barbershop with the evening's feature film
Cooling off the summer heat with *paletas y aguas frescas*
Broke down businesses flourish
Condemned houses root like cacti
Littering this stretch of urban decline
Big money having moved out long ago
Everyone going somewhere slow & fast
As if there was somewhere to get to
This part of the city that never
Got past itself thrusts
Out a bony hand like a panhandler in hopes
Of snagging something to hold on to

3

All brands of Christianity stake their claim
In the heart of this vampire
Churches abound on every block
*La Ultima Llamada* The Last Call
Looks more cantina than a place to worship
The congregants drunk on holy wine
Keeping time in tongues & song
I savor its double entendre

Love the humor it holds
The human-ness it evokes
The Potter's House the Basilica of the Little Flower
Historic Catholic shrine where the effigy
Of St. Teresa lies in a surreal state of sanctity
The road to heaven lined with unlit streets & pot holes
Bars of every kind to whet the flesh feed the soul
Offering salvation for those lost in this hell
The poor boxed in their misery
The churches rife with captive clientele


4


Down the way a lone woman scantily dressed
Alluring attire primed for sensual success
Waits for the flaming wheels of deliverance
To whizz her off into dystopia's delusion
Dante's tempestuous whirlwind to navigate
The desperate economy her life promotes
The meager wages necessity demands
That forces many to find the nightly fix
To make the day livable
Traffic signals blink faces blur
I shift gears ground the engine
'Til it growls like an angry stray
People remain chained
To the status quo unchanged
For centuries
I switch lanes slowdown
Every night unspooling footage for a PBS documentary
Minus cameras & film
I accelerate south toward Frío City Road
Gliding by signs of renovation that rise
Like weeds in crumbling concrete
The Biblio-Tech Library connects the
Less fortunate to the marvels of the worldwide web
The recently restored Brady Gardens presents
Affordable homes for the recently displaced
Mini Marts Dollar Trees taking root among the general rot
These streets I travel like in my youth
Looking for a way out realizing they were only

A way into myself knowing that the life out there
Flows inside of me here
Where I will always play a part
Coming or going
In this grand scheme lived out before my eyes
A very human theater without walls
Alive every night full of foible & folly
Until I too fade
Into the ever-swirling shades of night
Another concrete citizen of the streets
Not lined with imperial gold
No less priceless
That will outlast the rest of us

# Song for America

## XXXI

Just a word . . .

At the age of nine like bitter tonic
He swallowed the jagged letters
Of its acidic taste

1959 Houma Louisiana the summer
His mother shipped him off with
Tía Minerva Tío Carlos & daughters
His uncle rough necked the Gulf for oil
They lived in a trailer park among many other
Roughnecks mostly poor & white before the term
*Trailer trash* became a crass stereotype
A chic insult of a certain class

Tía Miné as she was known in the family
Brought a pink liquid lotion poured it
Over his skin & scrubbed his arms
Like sandpaper and said *to rub the brown away*
He didn't understand the ritual
But fully felt the unintended slur
As if his brownness was something
Less acceptable & dirty
& sent him off with Tommy Lee
White boy about his age

At the only movie theater in Ponchatrain
His uncle & his aunt having some business
To take care of must have surely let him go
Once inside the theater they bought a pickle each
& Tommy more reckless & daring
Scampered up to the *"n\*\*\*\*\*" balcony*
He said as natural as drawing breath

The word—stopped him in his tracks
Knew the term in English had no Spanish twin—
*Grr*-owled like an unleashed angry dog
Flashing its pointed teeth spraying its foul breath

Yet he tailed Tommy up the stairs unblinkingly
His eyes unaccustomed to unlit spaces
Scanned the room & saw a sea of dark faces staring back
Couples in embrace men women
Watching the newsreels of the day
No one said a word at the white boy & the brown one

Standing at the rail Tommy said *bite your pickle & spit it out*
He pointed down below & *watch*
So—they did several times—ran back down when
People started swearing squirming
Looking up to see what was going on some getting
Out their seats cursing calling for the ushers

Innocence ripped like the tears in his
Jeans by two snarling syllables

# Song for America

## XXXII

Aretha Franklin 1942- 2018, American singer

With all due R.E.S.P.E.C.T.

*Queen of Soul*
*Ultra-Singer*
*Hey Soul Sister*

Media tags to make people
Palatable or despicable
I—for one—don't do well
With titles or labels
Especially when it comes
To celebrity or cultural fads
Famous or infamous
I am not sure who deserves the designation
To front an entire group
But I know you rocked while you were here
& the space you occupied will be
Hard pressed to fill

*Get in the groove*
*And let the good times roll*

Your voice blared soul
& your soul surpassed the natural realm
I don't know where we all go
When we leave this place
That's been our home
But I'd like to believe
We've all been given
A little heap of heavenly hope
To share with our fellow refugees
Enjoy a while
A bit of what we once
Gave up or lost
Somewhere down the line

Knowing full well there's
Hell enough to pay
Along the way
What you do
With *just a little bit*
Is up to you

# Song for America

## XXXIII

*Tres* for Trino

Trinidad Sánchez, Jr., friend, mentor & fellow American poet, July 30, 2006

### 1

Firing off a
Casualty list
Each body a name
Pumped full of lead
Young men women children
Butchered on the red stroked
*Motor City* streets
Mimicking the sounds
Of Glocks & AK 47s
Echoing in the early hours
Of the grim-faced clock
The day littered
With the night's
Roll call of fatalities
Someone's son
Someone's daughter
The conservative bookstore
Crowd shaken to the core
Behind your bullet laced litany
That never fails to jolt
The sensibilities of those
Who wake & sleep in comfort
Pleading demanding
That we stand up

*Stop the violent madness*

As you calmly ease the trigger
Shift gears & with
A gentle guiding tone
Begin accentuating poems
About indigenous identity

Heritage social justice the struggle
For the common dignity of man
Even jalapeños find
Their rightful place in your poetry
& help us voice the possibilities
Dreaming big can bring
You espoused no sacred cows
Tore down prison bars fences
All was fair in the poetic war
Against inequality & bigotry
In a northern Yankee drawl
I once heard you propose
A question a young
Chicanita might suppose
About the color of her skin
& finish off with
An affirmative punctuated end

*God made you brown* mi'ja
*Because it was her favorite color*

That gave way to wild applause
Curious for *a home grown*
*Down home brown bro'*
Trinidad your verse
Still underscores
The necessary point
That helps us laugh
At our feeble selves
Gives us pause
Exhorting us to contemplate
The words other voices
Had to say
Martin Luther King Malcolm X
Mahatma Gandhi César Chávez
Excoriating hate
Declaimed by boundless poets
Proclaimed before audiences
From countless countries
Across the world

Denouncing tyranny
Lifting up humanity
Echoing from the mountain tops
Those words even now
The same words
That flow from your poems


2


The words from the lines
From the poems
In the books you wrote
Are like rain
Nourishing my roots
I carried the flame
At an early age
Knew it held truths
Mysteries too deep
To be hastily understood
& you valued above all
The power of words
The primitive origins
Of their sacred fire
Brother poet
Unassuming mentor
Guiding hand to my quest
Travelling together
The cities of our state
Bringing the bread of poetry
To break in conference rooms
Festivals bistros taverns
Bookstores book fairs
Universities backyard barbecues
Wherever there was need
Sowing understanding
Breaking barriers
Healing wounds
Cruelty makes
Kindling the spark
Of friendship that still refreshes

Worn out hearts
We grappled time for poetry
But time was not enough


3


We parted ways awhile
You kept the fight
In the community
Opening doors to previous
Difficult domains
I determined to reclaim
The American schoolyard
In the name of literacy
Kudos came our way
Yours literary promoting
Social justice & awareness
Mine for teaching
Adolescents words
Do make a difference
Then came the catastrophic
Call *Trino's had a stroke*
The worst news always
Routs the good
You faced the inevitable
Head on at Methodist Hospital
Where you almost defied the odds
& though you never raised
Your voice in song again
I felt you firmly grip my hand
As if to help me carry on
A reporter called for a quote
That made the news next day
& so bound as brothers are by blood
Words became our bond
Later I wrote Sonnet XCIII
For you though no one ever knew
Except once at a memorial feast
Set for you where *tu Reina*

Regina inscribed in your final book
*Time passes but true brothers don't*
You nod in signature black beret
Smile behind full brush moustache
I close the book place my right hand
As testament
& solemnly agree

# Song for America

## XXXIV

Split the people pit nation against nation
See the gaps get wider the years grow harder
The indigenous the immigrants the invasion
Orbiting the outskirts for survival
Monsters of our own imagination
The last piece of America divvied up
The dead dawn on the final frontier

The Furies unleash their rage
The Four Horsemen gallop across the page
With impunity an apocalyptic
Age unlike any other
The last vestiges of innocence lost

In mayhem's quicksand
Common courage carries the day
Maria with the sparkling smile
Dabs the tabletops at Rosa's Café
Believes *This is a good place*
Juan staffs the register at the corner store
Works two jobs says with gutsy laugh
*No hay más there's nothing more*

The borderline brown shades of those who
Pave the streets & highways
Arms & hands bronzed
By summer's sizzling heat
To make ends meet
Belief bears the pain with every clod & clunk
Of concrete they break
Nameless others who can't complain
Stomach the wrath & rain

See them as you pass by on the way
To where you feel snug & safe
Look into their eyes

Feel their isolation
Listen to the threadbare conversation
Bare minimal wage

Scrapping for survival
Such small consolation

Turn your gaze away
The dreaded fear
With a sackful of woe
On its tattered back is here

The face of the America
We thought we knew
At the front door
The future once—the rave of yesterday

# Song for America

## XXXV

### on certain issues of the day

Labels—I detest
Tags categorically pin people down
Into less than human groups
Like insects in a perverse collection
To be viewed inspected isolated
Behind a protective glass
That might infect the rest
*Economically disadvantaged at risk*
*Aliens invaders illegals*
Like having a nickname you hate
Once you're tagged—you're it
The sun sows not hate
The moon parcels not its light
The stars rain down a brimful
Without prejudice
All inhale & exhale a single breath
Each is granted a single panoramic dream
Answering to its one true name
The world shoulders every step
Knows each foot upon its back
No one is illegal
The land identifies its own
We're all supposed to be here
This is Home

# Song for America

## XXXVI

The man in the faux Lincoln hat
Wants to sell us trumpery
A country laced in frippery
Not the one we grew up in
Not the one we're living in
Where fathers mothers brothers uncles
Staked their flag & worked to dream a better day
A cause greater than they knew
But knew as right is true

The man in the faux Lincoln hat
Wants to sell a trumped-up story
Built on the quicksand of deceit
Sleight of hand coup d'état
A sham a scam
Where vice replaces virtue
Double dealing double talking
Dysfunctional dystopian
A rule of none &
Only one can fix the hoax

The man in the faux Lincoln hat
Wants an alienated plot
Of only *haves* no *have nots*
Built upon our backs
No room for me or you or us
A nation of mendacious hacks
A country of counterfeits
Where nothing works &
No one really fits

# Song for America

## XXXVII

*There will be time to prepare a face to meet the faces that you meet—*
The Love Song of J. Alfred Prufrock, T. S. Eliot

1.   America's Got Talent

*Dos cholos chistosos two crazy ass cholos*
Full of jokester camaraderie
Of the street variety
Dance & jive in line
For their 11 o'clock beer run
Tattooed to the gills
Bandanas tied no frills
Pay the store clerk Lorenzo behind
The counter with nickels & dimes
All the spare change hustled
From cash strapped customers just trying to get by
*I haven't partied in long time, esé*
Says the one with the blue bandana
Looking like he just got out of bed
They shuffle out like two hotwired versions
Of Cantinflas & Charlie Chaplin
Alcohol & mischief—the menu of the day
Lorenzo's a budding *star*
Tall striking looks would be cliché
Long light brown hair
Chestnut colored beard
Bordering a fair round face
Andrea Bocelli smile
Stands behind the cash register
At the corner store while I get
The daily news from the stack
Tells me he's pursuing a liberal arts

Degree maybe teach religion
What he should be doing
Strange but doesn't fit the theologian
Mold in these troubling times


2

Outside a tall elder black man
Distinguished bearing with a slight limp
Asks if I might spare .75¢
Says he's cold *Someone gave me this jacket*
I slip some cash into his hand
Tell him to be safe wondering
What brings him down these unkind streets
Careful not to stereotype
Why a man—any man—can't
Get up & walk anywhere in America
Without fueling suspicions or riling up recriminations
*Yeah* he echoes my advice *be safe*
Hobbles into Lorenzo's store
I drive away thinking of
How hard the times for young & older
Americans—not that I ever had it made—
Some on the threshold
Of their lives others at the finish line


3

Sliding up to a stop sign
I almost thump an indigent anciano
On a bike as he pedals
Right in front of my car
I've seen him before at the store
Wave him off he nods
Gives an indignant finger
Steers behind my car
Knowing I missed & not too happy
I drive away feeling strangely indicted

Guilty of attentive inattention
Cruel—the street rule—
One traffic sign away sits doom

4

At the corner of W. Southcross & New Laredo Highway
A homeless white woman lingers underneath a light pole
In the middle of the day
Bundled up against the coming cold
Shopping cart loaded with all her things
Bothering no one drags on a cigarette
Motions with her hands talks to the air
As if she were in her living room
& this the most natural thing to do

5

In front of a closed auto repair shop
A dark skinned white bearded
Small Mejicano face worn & leathery
Like a Hindu mendicant
Having renounced all possessions
Inert as a statue on Easter Island
Stares blankly at the passing cars
The odd suddenly seems familiar
Abnormal the *now* normal
Love—a prickly weed gripping
The concrete for survival—
Hope a luxury the poor can ill afford
A rickety house quietly rotting
Among crab grass
Towering wild weeds
A 60s hippie van
On cinder blocks rusted
Beyond repair
In a vacated lot
A front porch view—
State of the union

# Song for America

## XXXVIII

for Steven Craig Collins, American poet

For those born black brown poor
Boxed in the underbelly of utopia
Doomed to trawl for scraps
Poetry came to set the crooked straight
Break the barriers of brass
Split the bars of iron
Throw down all things cruel & hard

Poetry armed & dangerous
Stark & startling you declared
"I am the grandbaby of a 'Dream deferred'"
Yet undeterred seasoned in hell
You squared away
The truth like a cracked bell

Black's always been beautiful
But never more than in the poems you left
A friend called you "griot"—*djéle*
Traveling poet worker of wonder words

I agree with his decree
You published a book in '97
Later dropped out disappeared
Shades of Chatterton Villon Rimbaud
Wunderkinds restless spirits
Born to burn at birth

Where do young poets go
The bonfires of their poems
Smoldering in the ashes of the present

They sometimes grow old
Many older ones grow cold

New stars rise
Others finally wear themselves out & die
I was plundering the shelves for poetry
When your book *pluckin' corn on the sabbath*
Jumped out at me
Books like yours end up in the hands
Of those that need them
Cross the dearth of the years
To get here
Your words as clear now
As when you spoke them first aloud
Pry the conscience like a crow bar
Pummel our comfort zones
Punch to the solar plexus
Of the prevalent mediocrity
No media marvel your calling cred—
Poetry purified like moonshine
Straight from the still of the streets

Still resonating with
Prophetic rage to temper deadly hate
That breeds like the bubonic plague
& though we've made some strides
Kicked that ticking time bomb down the line
We still have not arrived
We just can't seem to get a grip
Treat each other with respect
Reject the racial animosity
That feeds upon our souls
& mucks up our beliefs
Retreat is what we do best
Fall back & re-ignite

The same old civil war
The same old tired petty fight for color
We should have dealt *those stanks*
A fatal blow

& when our vision clears
& we finally see
Wretched chains broken at our feet
SING unreservedly with jubilee
*Set free*
*Set free*
*Finally set free*

# Song for America

## XXXIX

### The What We Want Blues

*Imagine* this John

It seems WAR we've been made for
After all is said & done
We're right back where
We started from

It seems that peace is for the weak
& those that turn the other cheek
We'll never learn to beat back hate
So let's be real and feed our rage

I hate you & you hate me
We've learned our lessons well
You bomb me & I'll bomb you
We'll send it all to hell

War's coming what we want
Why pretend or hesitate
Let's just vote to end it all
Set the record straight

Preachers preach damnation
Presidents keep score
No one needs a reason
When All we want is war

Politicians polarize
Maximize their profits
Pray to god on Sunday
Double line their pockets

Prophets prophesy ancient doom
Poets scream their final breath
Why talk of liberty & justice
When all we want is death

M.L.K. said *I have a dream*
*The dream is over* Lennon's dead

I hate you & you hate me
We've learned our lessons well
You bomb me I'll bomb you
Let's send it all to hell

# Song for America

## XL

*At St. Stephen's*

### 1

Streaming live from the street
Brained by billboards ads
Auto sales by the score
Grocery stores packed by the dozen
Into cramped aisles of concrete lots
Industrial parks rusting behind tin fences
*We buy scrap metal* the irony of iron
Ice machines proclaiming
*Más hielo por su dinero*
Twice the ice in two languages
To sweeten the deal
Money's universal tongue
Dentistry next to bakery
Everywhere words selling telling
The marvels of barrio *crap-italism*
Eking out a living from leftover scraps
Hard poetry extracted from the landscape

### 2

At 3 a.m. silence's twisted logic
The wrestling wrangling before
The avenging angel of light
Is this what the dead see
Voices devoid of faces that intrude
With their incessant badgering
The mind slipping quickly down the streets
Void of life images coalesce in the dark
Mother surfaces in her final throes

Eyes staring wide open at
The upper corner of her room
Slightly nodding as to agree
With someone unseen come
To whisk her home her final words
A fitting poem
*Me voy me voy I am leaving*
& so for solace I sought the streets
& found camaraderie
A kinship with the lost
A lasting thirst & hunger
That cannot feed the flesh
A longing for the inarticulate
A wresting of words from nothingness
Before the grand finale
The last crossing
No papers needed no ID
All paperwork filed beforehand
Everything you owned disowned


3

We like to say—
We've forgiven forgotten
All the slights hurt suffering
Mistakes incurred of our own making
Pain inflicted by others
Heaped upon by the dogged years
Put them all behind us
With one wide magnanimous sweep
Of our benevolent hands
Until misery like a mendicant
Arrives arbitrarily dragging
A new arm load of misfortune like a bag
Of dirty laundry to our door

4

At San Fernando Cemetery
At the site of my three ghosts
Their gravesite undisturbed untended
Overgrown with weeds
Great Grandmother Guadalupe
Tío Joe Aunt Magdalena
Entombed together at the end
In such a little plot
How hard life must have been
In this country already steps behind
At the start of their century
Mexican immigrants
Poor undereducated scrapping
For bits of bliss
From San Luis Potosi
To the Tejas frontier
To their home on N. Frío Street
Did they find what they came for
As they carried forth their part
Never having much of anything
But troubles all their lives
The stars too remote to reach
Their dreams ground in dirt
How they passed through this world
Heads bowed low unnoticed
Unappreciated unheralded
Like raggedy clouds dissolving overhead
Shadows barely scraping ground
Having disembarked the train of destiny

5

I stand before St. Stephen's Church
Named for the first Christian martyr
Where I served the faith as a boy
Where Father Charles honored Mother

With a poem I wrote for her funerary mass
His voice wavering with each pause
Each word loosening chips of shattered heart
The stage set for so many others
Its doors now shut victim
Of dwindling attendance
A sick & aging parish no longer able
To sustain the saint
Of all the journeys one must make
The hardest one is toward *self*
I don't want to be confined in tight spaces
Buried dead or alive in one dark place
I've had enough of being kept down
Closed in counted out
I've left my books poems journals papers in a box
Scatter my thoughts over earth
Look for me in the wind
*Hay nos vemos San Antonio*

# Song for America

## XLI

### & the Winner is…

How does one select an image from the vast vault
Of the dead to spell the times
How can we single one out of so many no doubt
Pulitzer Prize winning photographs no one can deny

Native Americans rounded up into reservations
Blacks lynched in Mississippi
Vietnamese villagers napalmed at My Lai
Jewish corpses piled high at Auschwitz
Brown children caged in American concentrated camps
Only amp the devastation

3-year-old Aylan Kurdi
Drowned along with his mother Rehan & his 5-year-old brother Galip
Syrian refugees trying to reach the Greek Island of Kos
His tiny body washed ashore as if he'd been cradled to sleep
In the smothering arms of the sea

Oscar Ramirez 25 daughter Valeria 23 months swimming
The Río Grande between Matamoros Mexico & Brownsville Texas
Rumors of a better life found drowned
Rustling face down in the reeds on the other side
Her little body tucked headfirst into his shirt
To make sure she wasn't swept away
From a father's desperate grip
Images ingrained in the public eye
Conscience no longer pricked
You would think it would come easily
Such catastrophes condemned

Nothing propels nations into action
Reactions dulled par for playing politics
Token condolences
Parroted prayers
That never get off the ground
Unable to penetrate heaven's iron dome
Tragedy after tragedy until travesty
Becomes misfortune's fool

Calamity loses its effect
& words become defective

# Song for America

## XLII

*Breaking News from the home front*

While you pay the rent
While you order breakfast lunch dinner
While you wait in the grocery line
While you haggle for a new car
While you water the lawn
While you take out the trash
While you settle in for the latest unsettling news

Brown children languish in detention cages
Men women seeking refuge herded like cattle
The plight of the stranger perverted
Black Americans X-ed out for X reasons
Churches synagogues mosques temples torched
Overcrowded jails overflow with human capital

As the headlines run
Hour after hour
Day after day
Like the rolling marquee in Times Square
Echoing images of the past
A constant marker of where we are today

The flag dies half staff
The approaching end
Of all who fought for it
Of all it ever stood for

Shoot the stars out of the blue
Rip the red stripes the blood-soaked fabric of liberty
Play "Taps" for democracy

See the cortège to its destination
Bury its heart in Washington DC

Follow on Facebook
Snapchat
Instagram
TikTok
Youtube

You will never dream it like this
You will not see it again
You had to have been there
You had to have lived it
You had to have had a stake in it

# Song for America

## XLIII

### Chickens Among Wolves

1

*This will be our trail of tears*
*Esta será el sendero de nuestras lágrimas*
*The story we will tell our children*
*La historia que les diremos a nuestros hijos*
*Nothing will be left of our passing*
*Nada quedará de nuestros pasos*
*Even the tracks of our journey will disappear*
*Hasta las huellas de nuestra jornada desaparecerán*

Bodies washed ashore
Water bottles scattered over parched earth
A child's faded red sneaker a left foot boot curled up
Like a dried tongue strewn about the scrub
Strips of colored cloth caught in the bramble
Like battered flags flopping in defeat
Bleached bones bared by
Wind & weather
Empty backpacks gutted like prey

Listen you can almost hear
The frayed voices of the dispossessed
As they prod through dense
Thorny cactus & mesquite
With sweat & dread
Fear the daily bread of their torment
Felt in both directions
Leaving peril behind
Looking ahead for America
Stories of hope of brighter days of better times
Plática—conversation—you'd hear around
The dinner table if you were home
The silence strangling out here

On the fringes—no man's land—among
Armed men & cascabeles diamondbacks
A quick stop now *run*

2

*When I get to Chicago my sister says*
*I can work at her restaurant*
*When I get to Houston I'll get a job in construction*
*I'll be able to send my kids to school*

*Who am I quien soy*
*Who have only known hard work*
*Scrubbing my life out of existence*
*For a miserly wage*
*Mopping sweeping washing the*
*Scum from other people's clothes*
*Collecting their trash cooking their meals*
*As if I was only born for their convenience*
*A chicken among wolves*
*Prey for their pleasure*
*A beast for all their burdens*

Constant contradictions
Grow deep & bitter roots in this place
Where so much blood has soiled the soul
Criminals murderers come to steal
Live off welfare what
They always say when they're
Too are afraid
Of losing their place

*Who am I Quien soy*
*Who have only known hard work*
*Scrubbing my life out of existence*
*For a miserly wage*
*Mopping sweeping washing the*
*Scum from other people's clothes*
*Collecting their trash cooking their meals*
*As if I was only born for their convenience*
*A chicken among wolves*

*Prey for their pleasure*
*A beast for all their burdens*

Seeking asylum then
Threatening to deport they
Separate children from parents
Confine them in caged pens
Raid places of employment
They snarl growl bark like dogs
'Go back to where you came from'

*Go home &*
*Don't come back*

The dream dead
El sueño muerto

# Song for America

## XLIV

*after* Sirach *Chapter 44*

*In Praise of Ungodly Men*

1 Let us now praise ungodly men each infamous in his time
2 Abominations in the eyes of the Most High since the days of old
3 Polluters of the land cowards for their incompetence
4 Pretentious in their prudence dissemblers in all things
5 Steadfast in their foolishness governors of gluttony
6 Authors skilled in deception forgers of lies
7 Composers of odious conceits equivocators par excellence
8 Tyrants entrenched in their avarice purveyors of their own platitudes
9 All inglorious in their time each arrogant in his day
10 Some have left behind a name and men recount their pompous deeds
11 But of others let there be no memory for when they ceased they ceased
as though they had not existed
12 Evil men whose exploits have not been forgotten
13 Their fortune remains in their families their legacy with their progeny
14 Through wickedness their iniquity endures
15 And for all time their infamy will last their depravity never blotted out
16 Let their bodies rot away though their names live on
17 At gatherings their scandals retold & the people proclaim their sins

# Song for America

## XLV

*For the children in American detention camps*

The stars are falling
Walking among us
Darkness consuming
The dim light they've
Left to give
The hour growing thin
The clock heavy with the past
A loaded gun at its temple
Love an aborted attempt—a vain substitute—
To stem death's success
Losing more than minutes
The soul sickly & paralytic
Tossed by the roadside
Of our disrupted dreams
&
We no longer see the road ahead

# Song for America

## XLVI

*Para los niños de la frontera*

Las estrellas caen
Caminando entre nosotros
La obscuridad consumiendo
La débil luz que les queda
Las horas adelgazan
El reloj cargado del ayer
Una pistola en la sien
El amor un intento abortado
—un substituto vano—detiene el éxito mortal
Perdiendo más que minutos
El alma enferma y paralítica
Tirado al lado del camino
De nuestros sueños interrumpidos
y
Ya no vemos el camino adelante

# Song for America

## XLVII

When The Beatles performed for the last time
January 1969 atop their Abbey Road Studio
Things had already gone helter skelter
I had not yet turned nineteen
The deaths of JFK MLK Malcolm X
still festered in the nation's wounds
The Vietnam War was raging
Across America's tv screens
Every channel replayed the carnage
While we gawked in disbelief
As Dan Rather reported on the rising
Casualties from jungles we only read
About in books
I escaped the televised lottery draft
My birthday checking in at #281

Teen years bucked like a rocket
I barely had time to breathe
Ms. Meynard my senior year counselor
Suggested I seek a career in journalism writing or teaching
—*your verbal skills are good enough* she said—
I scoffed at the latter having pretty much
Dismissed my teachers as dull & uninspiring
Teaching from texts I had no interest in
Except for British Lit & Señorita Vazquez my Spanish IV teacher
Who survived my wrath due to the fact she didn't know
What to do with me & Humberto Martinez since we had
The highest scores of anyone in her senior class
She brought a stack of Spanish novels & directed us
To read as many as we could then submit written reports
& "stay out of trouble"

She closed the classroom door & left us alone
To comb the Golden Age of Spain
Unable to refrain from laughing
At our literary luck
For the rest of the semester

Friends came home in body bags
Friends came home on crutches
Some came back in one piece
Some came without limbs
Some never came home again

I'll never forget the look on Mother's face
When the Army recruiter arrived at our house
To pluck my brother Robert
An unlucky-lucky lotto winner
I felt disoriented disconnected
Our lives disrupted

The fires of discontent raging everywhere
Civil unrest civil rights city riots
Bob Dylan twanging *the times they are a-changing*
The Beatles cranking *Revolution*

The song of napalm topping all the charts

# Song for America

## XLVIII

For the children of Uvalde & their teachers

*Everybody's got a pistol everybody's got .45*
*The philosophy seems to be at least as near as I can see*
*When all the other folks give up theirs I'll give up mine*

Poet Gil Scott shook things up with those lines
But politics & partisans got people on the run
Arm teachers worship god with a loaded gun
AR 15 ok at 17 & all the weapons in between
NRA jiggles jingles to state their case
*A good guy with a gun stops a bad guy with a gun*
& the homespun jive runs amok to defend a deadly right
Shout it out shoot it out school zones kill zones
Second Amendment trumps debate
Blast the eagle in a sea of bloody hate
Bomb the ballot box *coup d' etat*
Liquidate the nation's assets
In broad day light
You don't need an explanation
When everyone fears extermination
End the so-called *Constitution*
Beacon on the hill bunker hill
*Remember the Alamo come & take it*
*Give me liberty or give me death*
Bullets back bluster bluster breeds bigots
But you can't fake the grief stuffed caskets
A pyrrhic victory for civil defeat
Common good fails common sense
Common sense is of no consequence
& all our better angels bolt in disgrace

*Everybody's got a pistol everybody's got .45*
*The philosophy seems to be at least as near as I can see*
*When all the other folks give up theirs I'll give up mine*

# Song for America

## XLIX

So many refugees
Scrambling for cover
Rovers of the unforgiving streets
The semblance of a paradise lost
Nowhere to be found
A handsome middle eastern couple
Both tall pale complected oddly out of place
In manner speech & dress
She could be a Miriam
Madonna profile in long skirt
Neatly dressed provoking
Only wonder & a sense of calm distress
Chestnut hair pinned back
Cradling a young child in one arm
& a pizza box in the other
He young father
Hair cropped short at the
Sides curled on top
In the modern style
Boy about ten at his side
Holds a poster board that
Reads *need help*
*For family* & something
About *getting papers*
I think about approaching
If only to learn their tale
As a cop pulls over to their
Side questioning their plight
Fines them for panhandling
Confiscates the sign

They move off family in tow
I feel shame & vaguely confused
Not sure of what I could do
Petulant at the world
For the poem I must now pander

# Song for America

L

## Children of Stone

*for those who built the American Dream*

In hard soil riveted to the landscape
In the city of stone & steel forced like cattle
Into designated areas meted out by the new gods
Boxed in fixed borders we root along the byways highways
Slip in & out of your fortressed neighborhoods
Like shadows moving with the sun
Trim your finely sculpted lawns
Tend your impeccably manicured gardens
Our poverty not an act of leisure
But a symbol of survival we pay your taxes cut our losses
Nothing ends well if death's the end we have no time for mid-life crises
No time for books little poetry music a commodity we can't afford
Every day chisels another craggy line along our jagged faces
Every night steals one more dream from our children's sleep
No artist paints these black Madonnas floating in polluted pools
We are only one color never the right one
We turn & return to the brooding foreboding
Days our lives have become

# Song for America

## LI

Time magazine/Person of the Year 2024

The art of double-dealing freewheeling
Two-timing backstabbing double crossing cheating stealing
Treachery plus lechery
Hell is here on earth
& heaven has no wrath worth mining
A Faustian pact to seal the deal
Satanize your rivals
Falsify the facts
Alienate your allies
Cover all your tracks
Cage children in detention camps
Refuse the refugee
Humiliate the humblest
Praise the knave & all his kin
Vice is only virtuous sin
& sin is just the skin you're in
Provoke to provocation
Keep the controversial sensation
Ramp up the hateful diatribes
Polarize the country until
None can see truth behind the lies
For truth is just a firm avowal of a lie
Deflect deny inject the moment with an accusation
Couch an answer inside a dubious formulation
Repudiate today what was offered yesterday
& yesterday becomes a litany of oaths & curses
A host of horrible *Hosannas*
Venerate the venial
Vindicate the venal

The saints a company of village idiots
Replaced by cons felons & the villainous
The miracle the shifty prestidigitation
*Shall we gather at the river*
One god one nation master of deception
*Give us Barabbas We have no king but Caesar*

# Song for America

## LII

This is not 1920s Paris
The Lost Generation
Nor San Francisco 1950s
The Beat Generation
Not the *Champs-èlysèes*
But Zarzamora Street
Westside SA TX 2024
The X-ed Generation
Though at times I feel lost
Down these raw narrow streets
X patriate poet-X ed out in his own land
Story sidestepped in scandalous times
Home grown American with Mexican DNA
I pressed into the dream
Like cactus in desert thicket
Mesquite underneath sun's unforgiving rays
With its 15 minutes of fame
Not tethered to cartels
Don't care for green cards
Welfare rolls demographic data
Ethnic codes
No asylum-seeking plot to mine
No immigration line to cross
Don't need the literati to tell my tale
Not Hispanic Latinx Chicanx
Sanitized labels bureaucrats academics
Adopt to appropriate distinction
Appear cool with a liberal sophistication
I'll take AMEX AztEk
I'll be what I make
Destiny mine to check
Keep your labels
Your supercilious names
Your hate filled rhetoric
Your prejudicial games
I know who I am
Even if you don't

Born on this side
Nothing you can do
Don't need your vote
Like you need mine
Nothing to decide
It's my ride
To the end of the night
Don't tell me to go back
Where I came from
Because where I came
From is right here
Right now
Home is where my legs
Are standing & my flag
Was planted long before
You landed so
If you have anything of worth
To say
Say it with respect
For those who expect
So much more of you
For you who think much
More highly of yourself
Than we do for
Your deeds outdo your words
& the two do not equate
As the battered earth cries out
Turn around & see
The damage in your wake
The victims of your hate

# Song for America

## LIII

### Killing COVID-19

*Pandemics* befit language
& shake poetics of its cold old doldrums
Even the word sounds sanitized & safe
Distancing itself from the old-world view
*Plague*
*Contagion*
*Disease*
*Epidemic*

We've dealt with these Angels of Death before
The Bubonic Plague the Spanish Flu of 1918
Little children would jump rope reciting

*I had a little bird,*
*Its name was Enza.*
*I opened the window,*
*And in-flu-enza.*

Like ill-suited guests or shoddy strangers who show up
Unannounced knocking at the door waiting to
Be acknowledged admitted—we knew
They were around always loitering lingering
Like zealous zombies wandering our streets
Some in full view others emerge at sundown
Still a few on the periphery of our sight
We caught a glimpse & hoped they'd go away
Out of sight out of mind
Like the rag worn cliché
& now we tout the terms "social distancing"
"Sheltering in place" as if they were talismans
Magic spells or rituals to offset mal de ojo
The infamous evil eye

Stores today packed with people
Distancing themselves from others

Avoid contact of any kind
Wielding shopping carts like Achilles's shield
Stacked with high-priced milk & eggs
To ward off unexpected blows
From irate consumers unaccustomed
To the current custom
The former Presidente blames
The previous resident
Rejects responsibility
Saying *stay calm this will go away*
While he castigates the world
With all his wily twitters

Hospitals pale & all that ails
Schools shuttered
Businesses bail
Bars & restaurants keep
Customers at bay
The stock market drops
To historic lows
Workers laid off
The streets deserted
Stray dogs growl at passing shades
Bound for Dante's infernal flames
Everyone self-quarantines
In the cushy solace of solitude
Sterilized & cleansed
With nowhere else to go

# Song for America

## LIV

Dear John (Prine)
*Singer-Songwriter 8 April 2020*

There's a pink moon in the eastern sky
& John Prine has died
Coronavirus took a titan toll this night
Stole his breath stilled his voice
The world fallen in a dank dark place
His words shining their odd light
Down a deep abyss

John—I didn't know you
But your songs spoke a real truth
With folksy humor & a bit bizarre
Unordinary folks like me
Completely understood

I was living hand-to-mouth in those days
Studying for a degree
I had some talent but no real heart
I was plucking notes
Mimicking your modes
On my old six string Yamaha
Found I could carry a tune
Without the natural twang
Fancying myself a songwriter-poet
Thinking I might have a chance like you
A mailman from Illinois

You sang emptiness loneliness despair
Things I was acquainted with
I couldn't fathom how at 22 you
Could write a tune about growing old
Saying *Hello in There*
But having witnessed how age & time
Can ravage those you love
I knew where you were coming from

Your style was sheer *Americana* never quite mainstream
More like someone way on the inside looking out
But having lived the life you did
You sang reality in surreal terms
& I was hooked on the simple poetry in your words

Years later teaching ESL in junior high
To my Mexican kids using your songs
 *It's a Big Old Goofy World*
& *Onomatopoeia* to help them understand the nuances
We sang we clapped we laughed I hit replay
Got the point across you won the day

Your face so uncannily familiar
You looked more like us
Ojos estirados narrow eyes
Dark full mustache
Much like my Tío Beto
Who fought in the Korean War
We still don't know what for
You told us so much more about our lives
I could relate with no great compromise
You'd have been a perfect fit in our *familia*

Cancer & a bad lung couldn't bring you down
You kept singing through it all
So do one more for the road
Lift one from the soul
& let it go
Make it like you always did
Life never gets any easier
Just so people know
Like an *Angel from Montgomery*

*"To believe in this living
Is just a hard way to go"*

# Song for America

## LV

### La Dolce Vita
*(for Fellini)*

Like a pinch of sugar
A dash of sweetness—
Sprinkled on my choppy a.m. drive
To retrieve the early morning news
At the corner store where I pick up the latest
Accosted by caustic advertisements
Promising the sweet life
Plastered on dog-eared billboards
Puckered placards rumpled hand bills
From powdered milk to power drinks
Marlborough's to MD 2020
*Sometimes you just need a pair*
A slogan you can riff right off
& write a seemingly meaningless poem
Lotto tickets to *no loitering* signs
You can buy it all but don't
Consume your happiness on the premises
The premise being it's unlawful
Not to mention just plain awful
To risk life & limb for a few crumbs
Life being what's going on now
& now could always be much better
Though the murder rate rarely takes a break
—*Fellini jazz* comes streaming over
The university's FM trumpeting
Me to alpha-beta heights
Where letters meld into motion
Motion melts into emotion
& the disheveled woman at the corner

In tattered baggy jeans two sizes too big
Thumbs a ride ragging to herself cursing at the air
Clouds like cartoon balloons heavy & grey
With grief
Full of comic mischief offer some relief
Everyone on the street seems to know the way
I wait like a stranded cast away
Interpreting the trumpet notes
Annotating the message meant for me
Oblivious to the surrounding mess
The muse insisting on her own terms
Unwilling to negotiate any standoffs
Certainties or uncertainties
To be no longer her concern

Out of the darkest blue
Before the sun unfolds its brilliant plumage
Your text from beyond time past finds its way

*I dreamed of you last night—*
*It was nice to see your face—*

Glad to have made a cameo
In some fractured way
A face among the faceless images
That bombard us even in our sleep
Episodic feature films unspooled
From realities too remote to relink
I'm not Fellini but I too
Go out when the evening's day
Spreads out against the violet sky
Searching for *la dolce vita*
*La dulce vida* that always
Steps ever so slightly
Down the road
Ahead of me

# Song for America

## LVI

### Inner City Blues

Weatherman says
Another record-breaking
Heatwave
Headed our way looks like
We're all cooking now
Over a slow
Simmering fire
Grilled & charred
For the greedy
Gods At odds
With everything that's not
Nailed
To the floor
Disasters
Plastered
To forever after
Climate flames
In noxious fumes
Plagues reprise
Their ancient roles
To villainize the tottering planet
Like a Hieronymus Bosch
Triptych
Anthropomorphic
Insects bound for
Calamity's country
Scurry for cover
Their way back uncertain
The curtain dropping

Like a guillotine
Severing the haves from the have nots
Arctic glaciers
Melt like popsicles
On a stick
All things man-made
Shaken & falling
Failure—a sure bet
To win the lotto
Flags warped in patriotic
Propaganda
The body politick
Festering with lies
It's starting to feel less & less
Like we belong
& more than
Can survive

# Song for America

## LVII

### Los Ancianos/Ancestors

*All of us are migrating by instinct*—Diane Glancy, "Claiming Breath"


Crossing continents cactus & caliche
Dust pervasive trails stumbling
Down tracks like tumbleweed
Sun scrubbed pueblos mud baked paths
All but erased from the collective memory
By history's scouring hands
I follow the echoes of your passage—

Back to mid-19th century
Northeastern Mexico Coahuila
Nuevo Leon South Texas
You—
Simple men women of the land
Travelers over harsh terrain
Ahead border towns to traverse
Hard workers builders entrepreneurs
Poets singers artists obradores
Of every kind taking menial jobs
To feed the growing family line
Up through Monterey San Luis Potosi
Leaving La Patria y La Revolución
So as not to die of hunger
Caminando de pie on foot having heard
The promise of opportunity & work al norte

*No hay más que hacer*—so onto Tejas
You crossed that invisible plane—
The mythical demarcation of
Democracy's questionable domain
The blood tipped daggers of betrayal
Not yet dried on paper
The ignoble treaty Guadalupe Hidalgo rendered futile broken—

Pulling your progeny into the 20<sup>th</sup> century & beyond
Quiet men tending the needs at hand
Keeping the stories of sorrow & struggle
In the keyless vaults of a precarious tomorrow

You—Grandfathers—
Chips of flint
Obols common currency
Buried in anthropologic ash
Cairns marking a way into an
Impassable past
Solid as the pyramids of Teotihuacán
Guardians of remembrance
Silent chronicles of an odyssey
As yet untold unheralded unsung
No less important for its
Humblest origins
Your footsteps vanishing in
The yellow haze of oblivion

But the women—Amazonian hearted—abuelas madres comadres
Las vecinas—assumed the mantle
Las vocinas
The voices the speakers de los cuentos
De las cuentas caretakers of accounts
The goings & comings of all that
Transpired in the tenuous lives of family
They knew the count they kept the score
Sybils of the flames
Muses of memory
Tellers of tales
Oracles of truth of wisdom
The salt the spice the sustenance
El sabor of all our aspirations—
Without flinching in the face
Of desperation stood in the gap
Raised the banner of determination
Refusing to surrender turn back or
Give way to poverty's depravity

Siempre esperando
Hands clasped in expectation
Corazones entrelazados con esperanza
Hearts woven with hope

Only to face signs snarling
*No Dogs or Mexicans Allowed*
Home rooted in the heart
The Statue of Liberty stationed far
From border scrublands
Offering no solace
Grim fixed figure
Heart ringing hollow
Flameless torch
Gives no warmth
Standing idle—idol of a blurred ideal
A coppery indifference
Stamped across her iron frame
The children of the sun
Find humdrum comfort there

Other pressing concerns override
The need for tortillas & beans
The scraps of survival
National genocide
Violence mayhem
Scandals of every kind
Orders of the day
Impending apocalyptic gloom
Outweigh hunger's gnawing growl
The howling thirst for outrageous plots
Barbarous exploits on full display
The nation's destiny to date

I stare at the American flag
That draped a father's casket
Tri-cornered & presented
To his grieving widow for a life lost
Lives irrecoverable from the loss

I see the Mexican golden eagle & the American bald eagle

& think of how far we've come how much we've fought
For a plot of land that was always home
Price tags buried in the hard-pressed earth
The Ancianos that passed between both to get here
An eagle perched on cactus once pointed the Aztecs towards
A homeland Aztlán—before America—Aztlán
Two eagles over all two eagles over one
Home the place I'm standing on

# Song for America

## LVIII

*I Read the New York Times Today*

Good Friday—its cloak of sad Saturdays—
Settles over the city streets
A quirky stillness resides between
The strokes of Time's blade
& the chopping block of our existence
Light dazzles & dapples
Like Fr Hopkins gloriously
Caught once in a poem
Even if we only moved by instinct
To better view distinct things
Today children are trapped in cages
Ripped from their families
Used as political pawns by
Those who fear so much to lose
Parents vilified for their origins
A darker shade of pale criminal
I ask myself how much goodness
Have we let slip from our grasp
How many times have we chosen
Roads more widely traveled
Ignored the outstretched hand
Of one deemed less worthy
Spit on the beggar
Pit poor against poverty
So many Fridays come & gone
So much good undone

# Song for America

## LIX

Standing in line for my pound of barbacoa take out
A ritual spanning decades like the unofficial
Postal service motto through rain snow heat
The brutal winter storm the city just escaped
A momentary calm descending
Over the clientele of mostly elder Mejicanos
Following some instinctual call for the
Steamed beefy headed delicacy
My friend Jesse called *"tatema"*
& credited native people with its culinary origin
That called for burying a cabeza beef head in a burlap
Sack in the ground raked over with hot coals
& vigiled diligently until done

My turn arrives & the young lovely behind the counter
Takes my credit card asking *how my day goes*
As if we were close & customary friends
I say *good*
I hear the cook singing from the kitchen
Belting out an unfamiliar Spanish song
With verve & gusto
I say *Placido Domingo* she skips my quip
Wishes me *a peaceful Sunday too*
I walk out into the greyness of the day
Remembering it's Palm Sunday

# Song for America

## LX

at the corner store on the 4<sup>th</sup> of July

Small talk's not my forte
Though I can jibber-jabber
With the least of my brethren
At the corner store where
I often find poetry in the
Aisles among the shelves
Printed on ads placards
Posted to walls
Verbal gold in
The unlikeliest of places
Cans boxes packages
Objects of mundane art
A library of products
A literary supermarket
I scrounge around for poems
At the checkout line
Sunday's edition in hand
*Happy cuatro* I say
*In spite of all the bad news*
*It's still great to be an American*

Jumping in the shop keep can't resist
Puts down his mop stifles a curse
Unloads his weighted cargo

*Who would've thought an ice freeze in Texas*
*Could shut down the entire power grid*
*Hailstorms in May heavy rain in June*
*Flooding in July what's August gonna bring*
*Some mornings I don't want to get up*

*Been drinking more & more*
*I don't know* he lays it out *something's*
*Out there waiting*

I think of a Ray Bradbury story I read
*Been that way all my life*

Maybe he's an empath
I know what he means

*It's enough to drive a man to prayer*
Springs out of me like bubbly water
I sense his tension unspool like a taut spring
Feel his fear wish him well on my way out
He returns to a stringy old mop & a wet floor
I step outside wrestling with a poem

# Song for America

## LXI

Red as a fez
Cardinal doubles as a weathervane
Kamikaze crow arrows dipping over my car
I duck in sync with his mad dash
Laugh at the sudden instinctual move

Sunday in the barrio an oasis in a roiling sea
The church bell muffs its monolingual message
Homeless men women shove off on their appointed rounds
Some seemingly lost to reason & reality
But for different choices I might be among them
I feel a kinship with these unredeemed prodigies
Sons daughters who couldn't make heads from tails
Who let such stuff as dreams are made slip thru
Their outstretched hands unable to grasp
What was meant only for them
Sniffing here snooping there among the slop
Like rats in search of what they
Momentarily once glimpsed

The quest now dimmed by Time's relentless march
The passion quenched by shriveling age
A parade of bewildered souls each another Canterbury tale
Provoking a measured pity & a mendicant poetry

# Song for America

## LXII

Gray comfort yields verbal gold
In the unlikeliest of places
A shattering of Keats's egotistical sublime
Among rows of discarded junked cars
Twisted metal frames piles of useless
Tires basking in an uncommon autumn sun
The discards of an anti-Romantic age
The acrid smell of burning rubber
Overwhelms poetry aging badly blandly
Lines that draw blanks to rave reviews
The common man gives not a damn
For any of that literary claptrap
Give him his liquid dreams in a cold tin can
Lead him to the nearest taco stand
& he'll endure the harshest trials
The most disastrous storms life can induce
Leading like these dilapidated streets to deathly ends

# Song for America

## LXIII

*for Sonny*

Sonny's got the blues
*Sumthin's goin' on*
Tired of panhandling
For handouts & loose change
He's weathered well
Considering the streets
Another man's hell
Long white yellowing locks
Speckled ashy beard
Like a craggy old-time prophet
Maybe Isaiah maybe Elijah
The kind that wanders the walkways
Alleys talking to the air
*Still got sum*
*Jump in ma' step*
But these days he's slowing down
He stands outside the corner store
Not asking anything from anyone
Holds canned heat in his right hand
Fading blue flannel shirt fastens its fingers
Like a tourniquet about his thinning frame
Worn out cargo khaki shorts
A bit bedraggled at the knees
The weather's thought
To dip into the 30's this Sunday eve
Don't know where he'll end his day
I've seen him sweeping parking lots
Picking up cans collecting trash
Working just enough for a poor man's cure
Once he showed up with a cut

Over a badly bruised red left eye
*I hope you won that round I said*
He said *yes* & laughed it off
He's not interested in change or being saved
Just wants to live his own way
The hard blows life doles out
Are never easily softened or defined
Out here anything can go wrong
The right time is just up ahead
Not much left behind
Sonny's *blue* from so much *red*
The eternal clash covers every track
One street leads to another
The other where you're standing at
Sonny's got the blues
He ain't been back

# Song for America

## LXIV

*For Fauzia Azeem a.k.a. Qandeel Baloch, murdered Pakistani social star*

*In Pakistan 1,000 women are killed each year*
*For violating norms on love marriage and public behavior*
*"Honor killings" carried out by* family reports CNN.


Twerking on a tense high wire
In sexy attire high heels black nylons
Afraid to shake more than too much
Thereby sound the ancient siren
A modern girl hurtling toward her fate
Trying to hitch her wagon to a star under a sky of glass
Hoping to find her space in a country where women
Have no place but to be hitched assured of Facebook fame
Fifteen minutes in the eye of the hurricane

Breaking limits carved in stone
Standards dead set against you hard going all alone
*But it's too late to go back. I am beyond their control*
You admitted

Strangled by a *shamed* brother—*Waseem*—
Who could not deal with the hate your rising notoriety stirred
As if you were his hot commodity to negotiate

*Fauzia* though we change our names
To fit our latest billing as we curb our trendy
Taste for star struck fame while laboring in the dark
There's never been any doubt only lack of sense
Experience & Time to grow into ourselves

The internet ad baited my attention
Gave a link suggested *don't watch*
*Qandeel* I admit I bit
Viewed your video out of curiosity
To see what could provoke such madness
Not to gawk or satisfy a prurient interest

Found it by Western standards—a contradiction—
Tame & a bit tepid

I've seen my share of craziness here where even shame
Has lost its good name—by Eastern standards I'm sure—
But how does killing one's sister prove *honorable*
How does murder solve anything around this globe
That simply gets more difficult
To get as it slips out of our hold
At such a cold curious furious pitch

Like the aborted fetus found wrapped
In the crumpled pages of yesterday's news
Discarded in a nearby ditch
Clinging to one last shred of hope

# Song for America

## LXV

### The Camps of the Republic

History is a ragged prisoner
Dragged down the streets of the republic
Unrecognized like a prophet paraded
Through the riotous days
Of our hurried existences
Today
On the wall
Behind the cash register
At the Texas Meat Market
The Palestinian shop owner
Keeps a news photo of Arafat & Shimon Peres
The star of David tattooed
Like a reproach onto his forehead
A message from the *intifada*
On the American front
Thoughts of death camps
Genocide, the Middle East
Seething with open hatred
Cut like handcuffs
Through the early morning traffic
The rain sloppy & sloshy
Like the mind before wakening
Five male, Mexican citizens
Nervous as escaped convicts
Dart from the Union Pacific railyards
To a waiting black Suburban
That will haul them
Into the nightmare
Of free market economics

On National Public Radio
A proposal from the nation's capital
To erect a fence along the Texas border
Solves the immigration problem
The best democracy builds the next wall

For the record
Outside a local department store
Eli Montesino of Monterey
Was choke held to death
In front of his wife & daughters
By a twentieth century peace officer
Trained to enforce colonial law
One coroner said *Heart failure*
Another *Strangled*
The court said *Not Guilty*
When it comes to Mexican deaths
How many reports
Justify the verdict

Listen
There have been other holocausts
Other ghettos
Other killing fields
Not far from here
Seeped in unavenged blood
Unrecorded killings more brutal
Less important because skin
Must be sacrificed & subdued
For a righteous cause

This I know
The text of American history has many missing pages
Rips in the stars & stripes

Dark faces
Behind fences
Behind prisons
Behind borders

They should have been exotic birds
On an endangered species list

# Song for America

## LXVI

Poem to my country on the anniversary
of the incident at Guadalupe Hidalgo, Mexico

(February 2, 1848)


You grew imperial & majestic
Wings stretched as far as your
Dreams could reach
&
In the name of God Almighty
In a land seized from its native peoples
You pronounced manifest destiny
In a Machiavellian way:

*This land is my land*
*No longer your land*

Boundaries set
Borders pitched like army tents
Forever fixed
*X—ed*
& annexed
For a cool 15 million
Absolving all moral debt
Contracts signed
Every word legally binding

E pluribus unum

The deal polished like a sparkling jewel
On the prince's crown
Today
The wind blows the dust of memory
Across latitudes & longitudes
In this nation mapped & marked religiously
By degrees South to West

All calm on the northern front
The collective vision
Played up on television
Nightly news reports the war in
Media tags
*Invaders*
*Illegal aliens*
*Wetbacks*
*Undocumented immigrants*

Cross the frontier nightly
Like marauding bandidos
To get rich quick on meager wages
& green cards
The price for tortillas & beans
X-men, X-women
Black crosses staked on border patrol reports
Cold hard stats make
More manageable enemies
Of the state

But
Our brothers' blood
Cries out along the banks of the Rio Bravo
& the X
In the heart of Te**X**as
Is more than a signature
More than a mark
On a text
On file
In the home of the brave
In the land of the free

# Song for America

## LXVII

Like golden bison running along
The freeway burnished stalks
Of grass sway in the brisk winter wind
Shades of the great majestics that ruled the plains

One can almost hear the stamp & stomp of their hooves
Huge heavy horned heads bobbing as they snort
North to ancestral grounds undeterred by
Man's mad dash to undermine the planet

The great herds almost vanished in 1878
From the Southern grasslands
The Great Slaughter wiped out millions
Savaged for their hides their corpses
Rotted where they fell
To starve native tribes into submission

Sounds of the Lakota ghost dance
Permeate this sudden momentary flash
Drumbeats pace the human heart
Voices summon better days
& the coming of the buffalo

Some will say it's only wind
Riffling the winter grass
In the almanac of the land
Nothing is forgotten
There are things beyond love
For which there is no language

# Song for America

## LXVIII

*Borderland Beat*

Nine bodies dangling
From the border bridge
Nine bodies angling
In the early morning light
Five young men
Four young women
Targets of a tribal spat
Over who knows what
A cartel message brazenly
Clear as the sun rose bright
Nine lives cut off
A deadly price
Half-a-down payment
To balance someone's account
So the banner warning said in Spanish
Acid laced hate speedily delivered
Lives quickly dispatched
The journey of a lifetime
& no familiars to see them off
Who will spell the terror
Of those few moments
Before they fell gagged
Bound over the bridge
Sin abrazarse
Sin despedirse
De todo
Sin nada
Hanging like overripe fruit
For predators to pick apart
When they should have
Been getting ready for school
Skipping breakfast
Meeting friends
Doing what young people

Are apt to do
What are you to make of this
As you wake in your
Zone of comfort
Coffee percolating
Brewed to your predilection
Your Hamlet moment
Which pair of shoes
To help state your fashion taste
As you prepare your grand
Entrance on the world stage
Self-assured
Of brighter days

# Song for America

## LXIX

### Lines Written on Nogalitos Street

*"Of course, poverty is no crime" The Idiot, Fyodor Dostoevsky*

What more can we give
We've played out our
Lives upon these streets
Tintern Abbey far removed
Wordsworth's "splendor in the grass"
Only the struggle to arrive
The glory in survival
& what remains is what was
& what will be

Temperature skewers at 107°
A homeless Mejicano directly beneath
The freeway cozily couched on a burgundy
Faux leather sofa signaling with clenched fist
To cars & passersby
Unfazed by the day's worst weather ever
& a sudden rain of good fortune
Like winning the lottery
Stretched out on plush cushions of ease as if he
Were vacationing in lavish luxury on some
Exotic beachfront in Cancún or posing for an ad
In a store's showroom
How the sofa ended where it ended
Unclear but there it was
In the broad grilling August afternoon
For his own exclusive use openly & unabashedly
Comfortable on a south side city sidewalk

Underneath the freeway running west
Amid the rush of ominous traffic
The dizzying racket of buses squealing trucks
Grinding semi-rigs billowing exhaust
Suffocating the already gasping air
On the hottest summer day to date
His only concern—unexpected luck—
As people trundle about their daily business
Panhandlers risk the rush of angling for spare change
*Whatever you can give*
What *can* one give in desperate times
Car riding on a dime

A woman tends her SUV stalled
At the local library parking lot
Idling to keep it running
So she says the car stuffed with
All her worldly goods
Having lost her lease she's lost
While strangers shuffle by

Young woman clad in scant bikini black
Parading down the ways thó no swimming
Pool for miles one can understand her need
Elderly woman—amputee— grips her
Wheelchair for all she's worth as she rolls
Across the broiling intersection
The chair wobbles perilously backwards
Into traffic that scowls like a prowling shark

Los de abajo no longer underground
They've mainstreamed into the current conversation
Written into the social fabric of our world
You must laugh like Dostoevsky's idiot
At the tragic absurdity performed
Daily on the staged streets

To keep the deep deep bluez at bay
On a frypan Sunday coming down among
Tire & muffler shops *fix your flat in under 10*
While you wait & negotiate the going rate
Monica's beauty shop begs a facelift
Tommy's Seafood still fishing
By the freeway overpass
Used cars rusting in weedy lots
The pavement littered with broken glass
From the latest crash
The Ezee-Pawnshop cashing in
Unfettered by recessions or inflation
Barbacoa going fast at Tony's Tacos
All the taquerias serve it up & down the street
Get your tacos & your *Big Red* crush
To bottom out your cruda
Level off the raw hangover from last night

Head on down Nogalitos Street named for pecan trees
That left the scene unseen or the pecan seller & shellers
Up the road toward the now hip downtown arts district

There's a history here that bares its tattered soul
Rummaging the clutter
That defies romantic notions
Families settled along its stretch
Before highways & interstates
Came proselytizing thru touting urban restoration
La gente clawed & clutched to make a living
Mortgaged a home
Survived the dust & rot & prospered
What can one *give*
Flesh on fire souls on ice
The splendor of the world
Gone up in flames

Behind the Family Dollar
The cherry tree gives only what it can

# Song for America

## LXX

*Chronicle of a Poet Foretold*

Dreams—the stuff made of
Families migrating al otro lado
Before green gave way to greed
Scrambling a cruzar la frontera
Where misery lay in the mitigating scraps
& migas became contrived cuisine
On a New York culinary list—
South Texas abuzz
Emerged from the foggy fuzz
Of a global clash
Talk of *Axis Allies Hitler Nazis*
Words we'd learn much later on our own
Birthdays weddings funerals border trips
All too customary all too fast
Childhood a blur of fleeting comic strips
Sounds blending into a mélange of
Mariachis blaring trumpets weepy
Violins as if announcing the signature
Drama of our past & future lives
Trio Los Panchos with Edie Gormé
Cantinflas y Resortes on tv
We laughed until we cried
Javier Solis stylized *Sombras Nada Mas*
Mother turning back the years like pages in a book
Tía Andrea crooned along with Sarah Vaughan's
*My One & Only Love* ca. 1957
Rummaging thru Abuela's storage shed in Laredo
To her old RCA Victrola cranking up the old 78s
Tennessee Ernie Ford's down home bass-baritone

Like a minister he'd sing *Sixteen tons whaddya get*
& like a choir we'd answer
*Another day older & deeper in debt*
Intuiting what it all meant
Got a blast out of that

& then the sixties hurled into town
Like Hurricane Carla
Castro's Cuban missiles aimed at
Us & the 13 days of October '62
While we practiced ducking under
School desks as if metal & wood
Could protect us from an atom bomb
The likes of which leveled Hiroshima
& Nagasaki while the Belgian sisters of
The Immaculate Heart of Mary clutched
Their rosaries in holy dread
The 35th president assassinated '63 one day short
Of Mother's birthday & we
Hurried off to chapel promptly sent home
The killer killed before the nation's eyes
Could blink & we could breathe
Thanksgiving ended on my birthday
No moveable feast to celebrate then
The Beatles screeching twist & shout
I shook it up Mother shook her head
The Rolling Stones screamed no satisfaction
The drill-kill of junior high till high school graduation
Kissed my first girl on the Riverwalk by
The Texas Theater almost fell off the concrete bench
The Watts Riots going down in L.A. '65
RFK MLK shot down in cold blood in '68
The first-ever televised lottery draft
Winners bound for Vietnam
The fires of racism raging all around
Still fighting Lee & Lincoln's war

The smell of revolution & rebellion
Inching their way towards
Our little corner house on Calaveras Street
Curled up by the lamp shade
Herman Hesse's *Demian* in hand
Santana's *Black Magic Woman* on
The turntable needling deep grooves
Into the well-worn vinyl
Fizzling from overuse

Words lined up outside my jam-packed brain
Heart primed for flight
Burned my first joint tripping on the
Train tracks down Frío City Road
1969
What a time
For a fledgling poet

# Song for America

## LXXI

### Autumn Sonata

Incapable of change
The seasons persist on their
Appointed rounds
The dispossessed find refuge
In the streets solace in concrete
They no longer resemble their reflections
Their eyes drawn to the quick fix
The scent of dissolution draws them
Forward nearer to the open pit always
Before them
The impenitent sun a harsh task master
Prods them here & there
The moon merciful mother casts a
Sorrowful shade to light their path
How close we pass to the seemingly mad
Indifferent to their plight
Their wings dragging dust as they mill about
Immigrants of their own making in worn out
Shoes ill fitted clothes while the world
Slouches toward imagined utopias
Evening's grim cloak drops on deaf ears
City lights begin their slow ascent
The fallen descend like clockwork

# Song for America

## LXXII

### One for Camus

The age of absurdity
For the absurd man
Recently a poet said resignedly
*I have nothing to prove*
But having nothing to prove
Is proving something
Many walk the streets with their eyes
Closed unaware of the Paradise paradox
The daily wrenching irony one must confront
The crushing contradictions
On both side of the tracks
Ride the rails full throttle
The long train of doubts
Carting our imminent dilemmas
While we wait to pluck up our courage
Pick up our crosses
Cross our Rubicons climb our Golgothas
Storm our Bastilles blitz our Maginot Lines
Entangled broken fractured
A virtual Guernica like Picasso's
The earth swallows its own dead
The determined soul learns to navigate despair
Hope a figureless form we read in books
We hoped existed we could embrace
Even hell—at times—feels like heaven on earth

# Song for America

## LXXIII

### *I've Always Cared*

Enshrined in iconic cobalt blue by Oscar Galvan
Lady Liberty painted with a gentle hand & with all
The care of a loving mother
Cradles an immigrant child at her breast
Mantling the copper-colored child with her cloak for warmth
Bordered by a ripped chain-link fence
That has done it's best to keep out the unwanted

She stands at the gate of America
Where many have died been denied
Asylum assistance a helping hand
To lift them out of the quicksand of misery
Many arrested
Many turned away

She's come down from her pedestal
She does not turn her back
A gift from the artist
Reminds me that I too
Have been nurtured
That each of us is
One among millions
Granted asylum
Only travelers passing through

# Song for America

## LXXIV

### Charles Reznikoff gives witness

He steps out of his house
Closes the front door
Walks into the New York night
The air still as a portrait
In the National Gallery of Art
Cold as a blade against the throat
Wraps his overcoat snugly
Eyes ahead pen in hand

Chronicles the faceless
Men women children in cities scattered
Across the land
He will never meet & narrate in his book
*Testimony—a Recitative*
Spoken word poetry of his age
The violent incidents & injustices he will record
For the lengthy record
Will lie largely unread unrenowned
Forgotten American lit
Described by Paul Auster as "a poet of the eye"

America at the final stage of the 19<sup>th</sup>
& the border of the 20<sup>th</sup>
Civil War at its bloody end 1861-1865

Uncelebrated poet of loneliness
Of the streets peering into the cesspool of America
Early victim of brutal anti-Semitism
Of bareback poetry pared down
To its rusted nuts & bolts
Post Walt Whitman
No literary frills
Straight reportage from the school of the Objectivists
No flashy peacock verses

Gleaned from volumes of the *Federal Reporter*
From every state every year
Since the country's inception as a nation

*I culled the ones I felt would serve this narrative*
The daily lives & incidents of the working-class
Became the tale to tell
The characters everyday Americans
From every walk of life
A crime log
A police blotter
A litany of brutalities

From the South
A sixteen-year-old black teenager
Pushed from a moving train
Simply because he was in the
*"Whites Only" car*—the conductor and
The porter laughed
Continued on their rounds
As his body lay motionless on the tracks

From the North
A young boy runs up an embankment
To the railroad tracks only to find
A freight train broken apart
He waves to the part that is
Still moving only to be crushed
By the oncoming backside
Section of the train

From the West
Saw-mill accidents
Mining explosions
Train derailments
Leading to amputated limbs
Children working the mills
In slaughterhouses
Catastrophes of every sort
Common place

Murders for petty reasons
Splattered across the United States 1865 thru 1915

*Quite the feat as I look back*

The shaky stilts of democracy
Riveted in bloodshed as the nation
Progressed from its agrarian roots
To the iron of the industrial *rage*
The inner workings of the populace
Struggling to crawl out of the muck
Sprawling its barbaric gawp southward
Westward forward

Poetry of its burgeoning age
America's epic odyssey
A real tale without a hero
Only victims
Seeped in trails of blood

# Song for America

## LXXV

A godawful mess

When God gets up in the morning
After he's had his first cup of Joe
Views breaking news
Reads the New York Times
The Washington Post
Catches up on the world of sports
How America's team is doing
Who won the World Series
Glances over business & finance sections
Checks in on Wall Street
Scans Vanity Fair sees what's
Not hip this season
Surfs the X-Files (Scully's kind-a-cute)
Flips the obits peeps who's kicked the bucket
Skims a few movie trailers skips *The Exorcist*
Spies the new Three Stooges Xi Jinping Putin &
*My god what's that knuckle-head Kim Jong Un up to now*
*Nyuk nyuk nyuk* he

*Yes—the planet is in trouble*
He can feel the heat all the way up to high heaven
The oceans too (he's heard) are drying drop by drop
The air is so polluted
He can't see the high seas even on a clear day
He used to love fishing in the old days
After all he was a small village lad
Hated the trappings of the big cities
But what can he do
He's not Tony Soprano or Michael Corleone
He gave up the family business eons ago
Turned it over to you know…

God puts on his air pods
Turns up his favorite rock band
(You'd be surprised it's not The Beatles
Thó he finds *Revolution* grittier than *Imagine*)
& heads out to Gold's gym for a few reps

He's got a long day ahead of him
What with blessings to dole out
Prayers to hear petitions to approve or not
Religious political & personal scandals to investigate
Bored to the bone with politics
Always the same old wars & whimpering whines from
Those who should know better by now

God swears he built the original prototype
With a healthy dose of common sense
(I mean "Let there be light" right) Where did it all go
The followers bickered counseled copped out
Religion morphed into the *Thing From Another Planet*
The Don'ts turned the Do's on their head the Spirit
Of the whole damn thing scrapped along the way

*Seems the whole place has gone to Dante's hell*
*It's gonna take an act of God to fix this godawful*
*Mess*

# Song for America

## LXXVI

Blood cult mania drains
The open veins of Mexico
Coinage of carnage
Fashionable decadence
Cartel craze of blind barbarity
Murder without remorse
*Blood tourism* the Gross National Curse

Santa Muerte acolytes dealing border malice
Their anthem vengeance & disorder
Worshipping a brutal deity
More potent than cocaine
A crave for killing
Severing more than torsos
Souls waylaid without i.d.

A nation's spirit crazed
Cadavers piling up with punctuality
Their verdict set with the gravest spade
Maelstrom of mayhem grinding down
Apathy's blunt blade
The nation's debt slipping beyond grasp
The human heart dulled past feeling
This poem—
A garbled message texted
Back to the grand Conquest

# Song for America

## LXXVII

### Soda water Man Bluez

*Agua Coca eh-Sprite*
The old Mejicano hawked
From the Burlington parking lot
A measured beat with an accent
On the third "a"
A fluidness on how he
Pronounced *Agua*
Followed by the stronger stress
On the double "C's"
Then a flourish on the softer
Silibant "S"
He warmed himself in full sunlight
Weathered leathery face behind
A yellowed beard & handlebar moustache
A trapper hat with frayed brown flaps
The city having pulled out of
The hardest winter to date

Chanting *agua-cocá-eh-sprite*
To each budding customer
Exiting-entering the store
Threadbare bluesman of the parking lot
Echoing his one line refrain
A faithful battered ice chest
& a vigilant tired old shaggy dog
Lone companions
Of all his unknown days
By his side as he belted out
His bluezy incantation
*Agua-cocá-eh-sprite*

# Song for America

## LXXVIII

### Table Talk

A mentor speaks/for M.S.


She believed in the Muse
& warned against poetry
Slipping into rhetoric
Rhetoric seeping into poetry

She said *one can chose to be a writer*
*But poets are chosen*
Her words rang with the
Rightness of a church bell
But I kept them to myself
Feeling arrogance & vanity
Might creep in

A poet bears a great weight
—if one is—
*Hold on to your discontent*
*Fuel your drive*
*Fix your metaphors*
*Tune your epic*
*Make your myth*

# Song for America

## LXXIX

### Hope

Here's to flighty hope
For you have to have
That nondescript ambiguous expectation
That capricious whim
Defying all description
Ms. Emily D called *a thing with feathers*
Which I've never found perching outside my door
& no one's ever seen
Yet somehow seems to hover
In the furthest regions of our soul

The shady wish we seem to give anticipation
For a positive result
Having no proof to go on
But the hard work it took
To hopefully get done
Then cross our fingers superstitiously
Even sign religiously
For a pinpoint execution of our dreams
A burning for a better world
The end of bloodshed  or
At least a safe trip to the grocery store
The hundred-one- times you
Hoped to write the poem the story the novel
To find the dang thing gone

Here's hoping it comes back
But just in case
Leave the cage door slack

# Song for America

## LXXX

### Lady Liberty

à la Emily Dickinson

A glossy Hallmark souvenir
A lovely little thought
A postcard from the land
Of misplaced ideals

You seem quite content
A colossal cliché

It's not liberty
The haves prefer
But how to hold power
Over those that they deplore

# Song for America

## LXXXI

### Aliens

Numbers too staggering still we come
Crossing rivers oceans deserts
There is no end to our
Departures unscheduled arrivals
Untimed at all hours
There are no lines to stand in chairs to sit on
No border greeter for a welcomed stay or visit
No fence can hold us back or keep us out
What we are leaving or fleeing is not clear
Nameless assuming other lives wantonly unwanted
Wanting what the rest enjoy our motivation
So many soon there'll be no room
The stars our destination

# Song for America

## LXXXII

Olmec Chichimec Toltec Aztec
The forefathers *de nuestra gente*
The progenitors of our people
Buried under pyramids of oblivion


Like the great
Indigenous tribes of the plains
Elders vanish from our pages
Wisdom lost upon the age
Benevolence stretched to break
History badly etched & poorly erased

We move ahead
En masse
Between the frayed
Stars & flayed stripes

Migrating to some
Indistinct end
The way never clear
The future not what

It used to mean
The present lost to the past—
More than baggage
We must bear

The kind the cruel
The rich the poor
The ready
The unwary
Stand

Face to face
One to the other

Some fight
Some forfeit

The end is
The chosen way
We manage love
We legislate hate

There is no other race to conquer
No other frontiers to take
We must make what we've been given

# Acknowledgments

*"The American Dream"*, **Song for America VII** and *"Heavy Metal Man"*, **Song for America XXIV,** printed originally on the wall of the Delta Produce Company as part of the mural, *Good Bad & the Greedy*, commissioned by the San Antonio Cultural Arts Center, August 2002, ©2002 Fernando Esteban Flores (recently painted over without consultation of the SACA organization. Pictorial history of mural on file in the Fernando Esteban Flores archives.)

*San Antonio Current*, excerpt of **Song for America I,** Last Words section, article with poem excerpt, *Panoramic "Piedad"* by Wendi Kimura, (November 26-December 3, 2003)

*Americanos,* **Song for America II,** 12 poems published as a broadside titled "Americanos" to accompany 12 paintings by San Antonio artist, Luís López, a pictorial exhibit on the immigrant experience and the quest for the American Dream, © Spring 2010 Fernando Esteban Flores, on file in personal archives

*Voices de la Luna*, **Song for America XII** *"In Praise of the Second Amendment"* (15 October 2013, Vol. 6, No. 1), San Antonio, TX

*Jazzicity*, **Song for America XXVI,** published as a poster-broadside in celebration of National Poetry Month and Jazz Week on Trinity University's jazz FM station, 91.7, graphic design by San Antonio artist, ©2014 Sherron Huffman, April 2014

*Voices de la Luna,* **Song for America VIII,** "I Hear America Cringing", (15 October, 2014, Vol. 7, No. 1), San Antonio, Tx

*Lost Children of the River* (anthology), **Song for America XLVI** (para los niños de la frontera)**,** ©2016 The Raving Press, Gabriel H. Sanchez & Isaac Chavarria, editors

*Lost Children of the River* (anthology), **Song for America IX**, *"Which Way's Home"* ©2016 The Raving Press, Gabriel H. Sanchez & Isaac Chavarria, editors

*History Lesson,* **Song for America XXII**, performed at the Blue Star Theater, January 13, 2017 as part of Dream Week San Antonio, Advancing the Voices of Tolerance, Equality, & Diversity, dreamweek.org

*Bad Hombres and Nasty Women* (anthology), **Song for America, XVII**, ©2017 The Raving Press, Gabriel H. Sanchez & Isaac Chavarria, editors

*Poets Facing the Wall* (anthology), **Song for America, XXIII**, **XXV**, and **XXVIII**, ©2018 The Raving Press, Gabriel H. Sanchez & Isaac Chavarria, editors

*The Thing Itself,* **Song for America, VII**, (Our Lady of the Lake University, May 2018, issue 45), San Antonio, Tx

*The Thing Itself,* **Song for America, XLV**, (Our Lady of the Lake University, May 2018, issue 45), San Antonio, Tx

*Voces Cósmicas* (chapbook): *PO-EMES,* **Song for America LXXX,** "Lady Liberty" and **Song for America LXXXI**, "Aliens" , ©2019 Fernando E. Flores and Carlos Loera, series editors

*30 Poems for the Tricentennial: A Poetic Legacy (anthology),* **Song for America: V** *"Yo Soy San Antonio",* City of San Antonio Department of Arts &Culture and Gemini Ink Literary Center, April 2019, San Antonio, Tx

*Endlessly Rocking, Poems in Honor of Walt Whitman's 200$^{th}$ Birthday (anthology),* **Song for America VIII, "I Hear America Cringing",** and **Song for America XXV**, ©2019 Stan Galloway and Nicole Yurcaba, editors

**Song for America XXVI,** *"Jazzicity",* Fernando Esteban Flores performing his poem with the George Prado and the Regency Jazz Band at the Little Carver Theater, San Antonio, TX, virtual concert streamed live on Facebook and YouTube as part of the Trinity University's FM Jazz radio 91.7 South Texas Jazz Project, September 24, 2020

*Catch the Next Journal of Pedagogy & Ideas,* **Song for America LVII,** online journal, Fall 2021

*TEJASCOVIDO,* **Song for America LIII** "Killing COVID-19", https://www.tejascovido.com/blog/killingcovid19?fbclid=IwAR1nvd5zyt nWbSqcOJX0m4RNHIeRCvZmaEG5eFa8onrzXoDwzQr313XZA_w, April 21, 2020, online journal

*https://gnashingteethpublishing.com/song-for-america-xliii-by-fernando/,* **Song for America, XLIII,** online journal, 2022

*https://infrarrealistas.org/song-for-america/,* **Song for America, LII, LV, LVI,** online journal, 2022 *https://www.texaspoetryassignment.org/war-poems/song-for-americanbspxxi-memorial-day-memory,* **Song for America XXI,** online journal, March 7, 2022

*Yellow Flag Poems, Life in the Time of COVID-19,* (anthology) **Song for America LIV,** *"(Dear John)",* Jasmina Wellinghoff, Editor ©2022

*https://www.youtube.com/watch?v=Xa8ob1fUa4Y,* **Song for America LXII,** "Sonny's Got the Blues", performed by Fernando Esteban Flores along with the Mario Arias Project at Barnes & Noble Booksellers, Ingram Festival Shopping Center, San Antonio, TX, January 14, 2024

*AngerisaGift (anthology),* **Song for America LXXIII**, "I've always cared", Edward Vidaurre, Editor, January 2025

# About the Poet

***Fernando Esteban Flores*** is a native son of Tejas; graduate of the University of Texas at Austin with a Bachelor of Arts in English/Journalism and taught writing at several San Antonio secondary schools.

- Published in: *the San Antonio Express-News, the Houston Chronicle, the Houston Poetry Fest, Voices de la Luna, The Americas Review, The Texas Observer, The Thing Itself Journal (Our Lady of the Lake University), rogueagent journal (issue 25), Written with a Spoon: a Poet's Cookbook, Is This Forever or What?, Lost Children of the River, Bad Hombres and Nasty Women, Poets Facing the Wall* (The Raving Press), *Endlessly Rocking: Poems in Honor of Walt Whitman's 200$^{th}$ Birthday* (anthology), Stan Galloway and Nicole Yurcaba, Editors ©2019 Unbound Content, Englewood, NJ

- Nominated for a Pushcart Prize in poetry by the Maverick Press and Gnashing Teeth Publishing

- Published three books of poetry: ***Ragged Borders, Red Accordion Blues, & BloodSongs*** (one hundred and eleven poems in sonnet form along with 11 paintings by **SA artist, Luis Lopez**) available through Hijo del Sol Publishing

- Collaborated in 2011 with San Antonio **artist Luis Lopez** in a series of 14 paintings & 14 poems titled ***Americanos*** on the theme of immigration and what it means to be part of the fabric of America which was published in a limited broadside

- Selected for Gemini Ink's 2014-2015 writing mentorship program with Dr. Carmen Tafolla, San Antonio's first poet laureate & poet laureate of Texas

- Performed with well-known SA jazz musicians in a city funded program called *stART Poetricity Project*

- Received 2 Golden Apple *ExCEL* awards for excellence in teaching from KENS 5-TV (CBS affiliate)

- Chosen as a distinguished educator from Bexar County by Trinity University's, 2008 Trinity Prize Committee

- Archived at the Ozuna Learning Center & Library at Palo Alto College as well as the San Antonio Public Library's new Latino Collection (first floor)

- Received an *ELLA* award for 2018 and an *Arts & Letters* award 2019 from the San Antonio Public Library System and Friends of the San Antonio Library for his work in promoting creativity, literacy, education and outstanding contributions to the Artistic and Literary Community of San Antonio, Tx

- Selected in 2918-19 by the Department of Arts & Culture of the City of San Antonio, with support from Gemini Ink for his poem **Song for America V** (*Yo Soy San Antonio*) as one of 30 poem/poets to commemorate the City's Tricentennial anniversary.

- Founded of a group of eclectic seasoned and emerging poets, *Voces Cósmicas* who have been promoting poetry, art, and music at different venues throughout San Antonio since 2012

- Named Poetry Editor of the CTN Journal of Pedagogy & Creativity